Present on Earth

For more information about
Alternatives for Simple Living
Call anytime – 1-800-821-6153
or visit www.SimpleLiving.org

G-6021

Present on Earth

Worship resources on the life of Jesus

Iona Community
The Wild Goose Worship Group

GIA Publications, Inc.
Chicago

First published 2002

ISBN: 1-57999-196-3

Front cover: Graham Maule © 2002 Wild Goose Resource Group

Published and distributed in North America by
GIA Publications, Inc.
7404 S. Mason Ave., Chicago, IL 60638
www.giamusic.com

Contents

Introduction

Like its predecessors, CLOTH FOR THE CRADLE and STAGES ON THE WAY, this is an eclectic assortment of material. The two previous books focused on the beginning and ending of Jesus' earthly life. PRESENT ON EARTH is concerned with the years in between, with the encounters and conversations, the rumour and reputation, the moments of deep assurance and equally deep provocation which marked Jesus' three-year ministry.

And such a collection is necessary to supplement the others. For, in no small way, we can only understand the implications of the incarnation when we see the vulnerable intimacy which God faced in becoming human. And we cannot make sense of the cross unless we have some notion of the depth of Jesus' love and the hostility of his earthly antagonists.

So this book is for what the Church calls 'ordinary time' ... the weeks away from the major festivals when we look and listen to Jesus on the road and among his people.

There is a diversity of material ... short collects and responsive prayers, dialogues, monologues and extended scripts. Most of this material has not been published before, but it has developed over the years as our colleagues in the Wild Goose Worship Group have enabled new initiatives in liturgy, particularly in the west of Scotland.

Because all members of the group with one exception are lay people, we do not presume that ordained clergy will be the sole users of this material. Nor do we claim that what is written here is unchangeable. As local circumstances require, words and phrases may be changed, sections of any narrative may be omitted ... this especially when the book is used outside the United Kingdom.

It is our hope that in using this material, more than the intellect will respond to the message of the Gospel. For, truth to tell, Jesus was as interested in his followers' experience, intuition and imagination as he was in their theology. Salvation comes by right relationship, not by right doctrine, and Jesus is the right person.

John Bell
Graham Maule
Wild Goose Worship Group, September 2001

Using this book

There are six basic types of material in the book, each of which is indicated by a recurrent symbol.

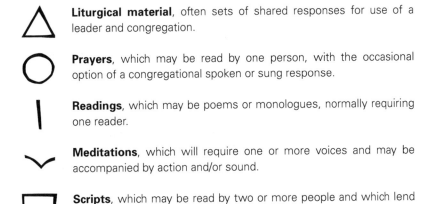

Liturgical material, often sets of shared responses for use of a leader and congregation.

Prayers, which may be read by one person, with the occasional option of a congregational spoken or sung response.

Readings, which may be poems or monologues, normally requiring one reader.

Meditations, which will require one or more voices and may be accompanied by action and/or sound.

Scripts, which may be read by two or more people and which lend themselves to dramatic presentation.

Symbolic actions, which enable the congregation to be actively engaged in the worship by physically moving round the building.

This material is arranged alphabetically except for its division into the three sections: Jesus himself, The company of Jesus and The way of Jesus.

It is envisaged that worship leaders will select materials from the book and incorporate them into acts of worship, rather than make a liturgy simply out of what is found here. Or it may be that in some of these resources leaders will see models which they might use to help devise their own materials.

However a word might be offered with respect to the different types of material found here.

Liturgical material is, by and large, meant to be shared by the whole congregation. Therefore these items should be printed or photocopied onto service sheets.

Prayers need not be seen by everyone. They are meant to be read in the hearing of the congregation. They should therefore be rehearsed aloud in advance of worship, so that all the words feel comfortable in the reader's mouth. To give someone a prayer at the last minute or to glance at the prayer the minute before you read it is insulting to God to whom the worship is offered and also to God's people on behalf of whom the prayer is said. Use of silence and sung or spoken congregational responses is encouraged where appropriate.

Readings may be suitable for some folk and not for others. As with prayers adequate rehearsal is required both in private and in the space where the reading will be delivered. The best readers are not those with contrived accents or drama school diplomas, but people who are prepared to be, for the moment, the mouth of God (when reading Scripture) or the representative of one of God's people (when reading a monologue). If the story or the poem or the words have gone through an individual's system several times, they will come out with conviction. If they have not done the rounds of his or her body, they will remain on the page.

While readings will usually be delivered facing a congregation, meditations need not happen in the same way. It has been our experience that people can engage imaginatively with meditative readings when they do not face the reader, but rather when the voice or voices come from the side or back as appropriate.

The feeling of voices coming from around cannot happen when microphones and amplifiers are used. These channel all sound through the speakers, irrespective of where the reader is standing. A natural acoustic is therefore preferable and most buildings can be so used, if the congregation or audience sit together towards the front and if readers speak with their backs to a solid wall which becomes a sounding board.

Of course, the 'T-position' lobby will remind us that there are hard of hearing people in church. There are also people of limited mobility who cannot take part in every symbolic action, as there are people with restricted vision, who cannot see what is happening at the front.

While it is important that their insights are heard, those who lobby for people with one disadvantage cannot rule or amend everything that happens in worship. To allow for a minimal degree of temporary discomfort is to demonstrate that kind of hospitality to others which is central to the Christian faith.

Scripts, like readings, do not require gifted performers. Many of the dialogues included here can simply be read by people standing in appropriate parts of the worship space which will not necessarily be at the front of, but may be in the midst of or around the periphery of, the seated congregation.

Symbolic actions should, in the main, be optional rather than obligatory. Not everyone feels easy about lighting a candle, or moving from their seat to a distant part of the church. This should be respected. People are usually quite happy for others to engage in such actions as long as they are not personally compelled.

When symbolic action is taking place, it is essential that any visuals used or created can be seen.

Just as we would like to encourage those who have purchased this book for its liturgical material to consider using some meditations or scripts, so we would encourage those who favour the latter also to try the former. There are too many false presumptions made about congregations by those who claim to 'know what they can take'. It has consistently surprised us to see high church Anglo-Catholics, who seem thirled to the Prayer Book, relaxing when a humorous dialogue is employed sensitively and in the right place, just as it has amused us to see diehard orange Protestants warm at the prospect of doing the 'papish' thing of lighting a candle.

Finally, we encourage users of this material to think about the space in which it is used. Up to a third of the difficulties people encounter in trying something new in worship has to do with the building in which they meet, yet architecture and seating are often last on our list of things to be considered.

When people sit far apart, not only will they find it difficult to sing, they will find it awkward to laugh and difficult to listen. There is something enabling about being part of a congregation as distinct from being apart from the congregation. Of course, there is a place for personal piety, but the corporate worship of God's people should not always be held ransom to the needs of individuals to have their own sacred space. Jesus advised such folk to use their closet.

Because most lay people do not spend their time prancing about chancels or speaking from lecterns, the more comfortable leaders can feel, in moving around the building or hearing their voice sound in it, the better.

There are lots of other things we would like to say, but too many words of advice might be more of a hindrance than a help. We therefore encourage you to enjoy using the material in the book.

Reproducing the material

Unless indicated otherwise, the material in PRESENT ON EARTH is copyright ©
Wild Goose Resource Group.

Permission to reproduce the material for one-off, *non-commercial* purposes (in
local worship or educational settings) is granted, free of charge, with the
purchase of this book. In these cases, the copyright source should be clearly
indicated as follows:

copyright © 2002 WGRG, Iona Community, Glasgow G2 3DH, Scotland.

If wishing to reproduce any of the material for commercial purposes (e.g. inclu-
sion in a book or recording for sale, or workshop material for which a fee is being
charged) permission must be sought in writing from the Wild Goose Resource
Group, 4th Floor, Savoy House, 140 Sauchiehall Street, Glasgow G2 3DH, UK.

Jesus himself

A glutton and a drunkard
Reading 1

This reading may preface a service of confirmation or commitment.

Ref: Matt.11:16–19; Lk.7:31–35

A glutton ...
and a drunkard ...
      that was what his critics called him
      when they saw the company he kept.

'Out of his mind' ...
      that was what his family remarked,
      when they heard the things he had to say.

'Don't go there' ...
      that is what one of his closest friends advised
      when he realised the danger
      that certainly lay ahead of him.

So to his critics, he said:
'I didn't come to call the righteous.'

And to his family, he said:
'Whoever does God's will
      is my mother and sister and brother.'

And to his friend, he said:
'Never mind the others. You follow me.'

He was Jesus Christ,
God in the flesh
reconciling the world to himself,
comforting and disturbing
so that the kingdom might come.

Sisters and brothers,
we have been brought by Christ into that Kingdom.
We are part of God's purpose,
not through our goodness,
but by God's grace.

Are you the contractor?
Prayer 1

Are you the contractor
who needs road-makers?

> Then why come to us
> who, drunk or sober,
> seldom walk in a straight line
> never mind prepare a straight path?

Are you the landscape gardener
determined to have flowers blooming in the desert?

> Then why come to us
> who know more about traffic and congestion
> than soil and nourishment?

Are you the dreamer
who believes that there are good days ahead
for the sightless and speechless,
the disabled and the demented?

> Then why entertain cynics
> with your vision of tomorrow?

Are you all these things
and also our God
who loves flawed people so much
that you can't wait to be with them?

> Then come, O Christ,
> and be among us.

Behold I stand at the door
Opening responses 1

Where possible, the Cantor's line should be sung unaccompanied.

Personnel: **Leader**
            Cantor

Ref: Rev.3:20

Leader: When the lights are on and the house is full,
                 and the laughter is easy
                 and all is well …
Cantor: Behold, I stand at the door and knock.

Be - hold, I stand at the door and knock.

Leader: When the lights are low and the house is still
                 and the talk is intense
                 and the air is full of wondering …
Cantor: Behold, I stand at the door and knock.

Leader: When the lights are off and the house is sad,
                 and the voice is troubled,
                 and nothing seems right …
Cantor: Behold, I stand at the door and knock.

Leader: And tonight,
                 always tonight,
                 as if there were no other people,
                 no other house,
                 no other door …
Cantor: Behold, I stand at the door and knock.

Leader: Come, Lord Jesus,
be our guest,
stay with us for day is ending.

Bring to our house your poverty
ALL: FOR THEN SHALL WE BE RICH.

Leader: Bring to our house your pain,
ALL: THAT SHARING IT,
WE MAY ALSO SHARE YOUR JOY.

Leader: Bring to our house your understanding of us,
ALL: THAT WE MAY BE FREED TO LEARN MORE OF YOU.

Leader: Bring to our house all those
who hurry or hirple (*hobble*) behind you,
ALL: THAT WE MAY MEET YOU AS THE SAVIOUR OF ALL.

Leader: Bring to our house your Holy Spirit,
ALL: THAT THIS MAY BE A CRADLE OF YOUR LOVE.

Leader: With friend,
with stranger,
with neighbour
and the well-known ones,
be among us tonight,
ALL: FOR THE DOORS OF OUR HOUSE WE OPEN,
AND THE DOORS OF OUR HEARTS WE LEAVE AJAR.

Behold the Lamb of God
Meditation 1

More often than not, the title of this meditation, which is a quotation from John's Gospel, is associated with the death of Jesus. But it was not the cross which John pointed to when he uttered these words; it was a stranger standing in a crowd.

Here we take four different pictures of Jesus and allow John's words to be associated with them, in order to feel that these words were true for the whole of Jesus' life and not just for its ending.

The principal reader, A, should be located in view of the congregation. The others should be on the periphery.

A suitable sung response might be BEHOLD THE LAMB OF GOD (from the COME ALL YOU PEOPLE collection).

Ref: Lk.2:25–35 (Simeon); Matt.13:53–58, Mk.6:1–6, Lk.4:16–30 (Jesus is rejected in Nazareth); Jn.1:29 (Behold the Lamb of God); Jn.14:6 (I am the Way)

Personnel: **A**
                 B
                 C
                 D
                 E

ALL: *(Sung response)*

A: Watched by shepherds,
he is lying in wool;
he is gurgling, laughing, crying,
wetting himself, wearying his mother.
It is a very old man who recognises
the very young baby.

B: This child has been chosen by God
for the destruction of some
and the salvation of many.

ALL: *(Sung response)*

A: He is speaking in the synagogue.
He is preaching from the prophets;
he is discovering how his words
do not please religious people.

C: Who does he think he is?

D: I think we've heard enough!

C: Show him the door!

D: Show him the hill!

ALL: *(Sung response)*

A: He is walking through the streets
which most decent folk avoid.
He is listening to the cries
of all those who go unheard.

B: Touch me, Jesus.

C: Heal me, Jesus.

D: Lord, let me see again.

B: Lord, make me well again.

E: Jesus, it's my child!

ALL: *(Sung response)*

A: He is confronting his fiercest critics.
They have tongues as sharp as razors.
They have plans
in case their tongues are not enough.

C: Why do you eat with the riff-raff?

D: Why do you call yourself God's son?

C: Why do you violate our traditions?

D: Why don't you take us seriously?

E: Judas? … Judas? … we've a job for you.

ALL: *(Sung response)*

A: This is him,
from Bethlehem to Bethany,
from Jerusalem to Jericho,
from Capernaum to Calvary,
from Golgotha to the grave,
from heaven to hell and back again;
saying,
'I am the Way … follow me.
I am the Truth … believe me.
I am the Life … receive me.'

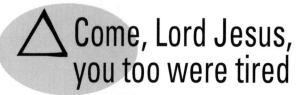

Come, Lord Jesus, you too were tired

Opening responses 2

Leader: Come, Lord Jesus,
you too were tired
when day was done;
you met your friends at evening time.

ALL: COME, LORD JESUS.

Leader: Come, Lord Jesus,
you too enjoyed
when nights drew on;
you told your tales at close of day.

ALL: COME, LORD JESUS.

Leader: Come, Lord Jesus,
you kindled faith
when lamps were low;
you opened scriptures,
broke the bread,
and shed your light
as darkness fell.

ALL: COME, LORD JESUS.
MEET US HERE.

He and she
Script 1

This script may be read by two people without actions and preferably to a soft guitar or piano accompaniment – SUMMERTIME is a particularly effective background tune. Reader A should be male and B female.

Personnel: **A**
             B

A: He was the son of refugees.
They hardly had time
to circumcise him as a baby
when the family had to go on the run.

B: She ... well,
nobody really knew her parents,
but most folk said
they came from the country.

A: At the age of twelve,
he ran away from his mother and father ...
the kind of thing a lot of boys that age do.
But he didn't run off
to get away from adults.
He did it to get closer to them.

B: She was probably fourteen
when she had her first period ...
a bit late
in comparison to most girls today,
but normal in those days.

A: There was a job waiting for him
when he was old enough.
He was an apprentice
in the family business.
It was a sort of
living-above-the-shop kind of existence.

B: It was probably when she was 17 …
or so they say …
that she became pregnant.
It created such a scandal
that she had to leave home …
so they say.

A: He didn't get married.
The way his job developed,
it would have been difficult.
He left home when he was thirty
and then went down in the estimation
of the people who had known him
since he was a boy.

B: Her husband died
long before retirement age,
so she was left depending on
what her family could earn
and latterly that wasn't very much.

A: He was popular with women,
but not because he was a bachelor
or a flirt.
It was because they felt safe in his company.
Even the girls people called 'loose women'
found that he understood them,
and wouldn't abuse them …
and that made a difference.

B: She never remarried.
She watched her son grow up,
then grow away.
But she was always surrounded
by young people.
Her son's friends often looked in
to make sure that she was all right.

A: His life came to a sticky end.
He became involved
with the wrong type of people.
He talked openly about things
that upset the peace.
He was a threat
to respectable and religious folk.

So they used their connections
and got rid of him.

At his death,
he was as naked as at his birth,
but observed by a different audience
which laughed and cursed.

B: She lived a long life,
but not without its ups and downs.

After losing her husband,
she was pestered by people
who wanted to talk about her family.
Her son had made a name for himself
and she suffered
because of his popularity and reputation.

Then came the day
when she saw
what no woman would ever want to witness ...
she saw the child
who had sucked at her breast,
with a fatal wound in his.

(Here any music stops)

A: His name was Jesus.

B: Her name was Mary.

He was present

Meditation 2

A simple dialogue which reflects on the ministry of Jesus.

Personnel: **A**
B

A: He was present in the temple,

B: but not just in the temple ...

He was present
where women made bread in the kitchen
and when women mended clothes in the sun,
so that he could find the language
with which to tell bakers and menders
about God's kingdom.

A: He was present in the synagogue,

B: but not just in the synagogue ...

He was present where farmers sowed fields,
harvested crops and hired labourers,
so that he could find the language
to let farmers and farm-hands
know what God intended.

A: He was present in an upstairs room,

B: but not just in one upstairs room
or at one special dinner.

He ate in numerous houses,
told stories at table,
brought in uninvited guests,
upset his hosts,
and was called a glutton and a drunkard:
... and all this so that the marginalised
might sample heaven's hospitality.

A: He was present in the garden,

B: but not just one garden.

He admired the gracefulness of growing things,
listened to birds,
watched sunsets,
and spent times on the hills alone
communing with his maker
while nature communed with hers.

A: He was present on the cross,

B: but only because he had been present
at other crossroads …

scandalously present with a woman at a well,
argumentatively present in a circle of legalists,
gregariously present at the wedding of a neighbour,
angrily present at the grave of a friend.

He was present on the cross
because his presence was unwanted.

A: He was present in the grave
to dust the fear from death.

B: He is present now in heaven
to be everywhere on earth.

I did not know his name

Reading 2

This reading may be appropriate as a prelude to the sacrament of Holy Communion.

Ref: Lk.19:1-10 (Zacchaeus)

I did not know his name
when he said, 'Come,'
and took my arm in his
and led me to my gate,
as if the house were his and I the guest.

I did not know his name
when he said, 'Listen,'
and spoke of other folk
I never knew
but who were soon to come and knock my door.

I did not know his name
when he said mine,
and asked for loaves of bread,
a glass of wine
and two small copper coins
for one old dear who'd just arrived.

I did not know his name
when he said, 'Take,'
and at my table, with his friends,
he broke a roll and shared his glass,
and said, 'This is for you,'
and sang a love song to us all.

I never knew his name
until he rose to leave,
and kissed me on the brow,
and said, 'I'm with you always now.'
I said, 'My Lord.'
He keeps his word.

If we met you, Jesus Christ
Prayer 2

If we met you, Jesus Christ,
we might not think that you were on a mission.

Your talk would be of common and curious things:
salt, dough,
lost lambs, lost coins,
paying taxes, hosting a meal,
wise virgins, and foolish house-builders.

We would not know you were on a mission,
we would think you were making sense of life,
lighting up the ordinary, identifying the truth.

When next you look with compassion on the world
and need mission done in your way,
Lord, send us.
AMEN.

In quietness and darkness
Opening responses 3

During these responses, four candles may be lit around the worship area or, if preferred, be lit within the central worship area. Alternatively, candles may be omitted and a short sung response, such as ADORAMUS TE, DOMINE (Taizé) or JESUS CHRIST, JESUS CHRIST (from THERE IS ONE AMONG US) may be sung at the points indicated.

Ref: Jn.1:4–5 (the Word as source of life); 8:12, 9:5, 12:35–36, 12:46 (the light of the world); 1 Cor.12:12–13, Gal.3:28, Col.3:11 (neither Jew nor Gentile)

Leader: In quietness and in darkness,
in peace and in confusion,
Jesus Christ wants to make his home
and meet his friends.

He is the Light of Life:
ALL: HE IS THE HOPE FOR THE WORLD.

Leader: (As the first candle is lit)
In him there is neither Jew nor Gentile,
neither Protestant nor Catholic –
ALL: ALL ARE ONE IN JESUS CHRIST.
Leader: He is the Light of Life:
ALL: HE IS THE HOPE FOR THE WORLD.

(Optional sung response)

Leader: (As the second candle is lit)
In him there is neither black nor white,
neither First World nor Third World –
ALL: ALL ARE ONE IN JESUS CHRIST.
Leader: He is the Light of Life:
ALL: HE IS THE HOPE FOR THE WORLD.

(Optional sung response)

Leader:	*(As the third candle is lit)* In him there is neither male nor female, neither master nor servant –
ALL:	ALL ARE ONE IN JESUS CHRIST.
Leader:	He is the Light of Life:
ALL:	HE IS THE HOPE FOR THE WORLD.

(Optional sung response)

Leader:	*(As the fourth candle is lit)* In him there is neither rich nor poor, neither working class nor middle class –
ALL:	ALL ARE ONE IN JESUS CHRIST.
Leader:	He is the Light of Life:
ALL:	HE IS THE HOPE FOR THE WORLD.

(Optional sung response)

Jesus said, 'I am the Way'
Meditation 3

After each section it may be appropriate to sing a KYRIE or other penitential text in response.

Ref: Jn.14:6

Personnel: **A**
            B

A: Jesus said,
'I am the Way,'
'I am the Truth,'
'I am the Life.'

B: When the Way becomes awkward,
and the going gets tough,
the tough get going,
they choose a different direction
and end up crucifying the Way.

A: When you said,
'Come, and don't bring anything with you,'
we thought you were only joking.

When you led us away from security
into the world of questions
and controversy and hard choices,
we thought you were off your head.

When you led us to meet and to touch
and to call as friends:
the sick folk and the scary folk
and all those we'd rather spit on
than shake hands with,
then we knew it was time,
time to change direction,
time to crucify the Way.

ALL: *(Sung response)*

B: When the Truth becomes hard to hear
we gradually become deaf.
We find lies so comfortable to believe
and end up crucifying the Truth.

A: When you said that God was here and not there,
we questioned your eyesight.

When you said that life was about giving and not getting,
we wondered if we had heard correctly.

When you said that in and through us your kingdom would come,
we knew you had picked the wrong people.

We knew it was time,
time to believe lies,
time to crucify the Truth.

ALL: *(Sung response)*

B: When Life becomes too demanding,
we run away from the demands.
We play with things bent on destruction
and end up crucifying Life.

A: When you said,
'Put down your sword'
and 'Turn the other cheek,'
we thought you were naive, soft in the head.

When you said,
'Don't worry about what to wear or what to eat,'
we thought you must be hallucinating.

And when you said,
'It's only when you lay down your life
that you receive it again,
we knew it was time,
time to let you take up the cross,
yourself.

ALL: *(Sung response)*

B: And yet you still love us.
You still love us and say,
'Follow me.'

We do not understand you, Jesus Christ,
nor will we, if we stay away.

Oh, draw us close to you ...
right to the end,
and through the end,
to your new beginning.

ALL: AMEN.

Our image of Jesus
Script 2

A is a blustering pompous character. B is more down to earth and a little snide. Towards the end, as A gets more explosive, B gets more quiet and serious. The readers should almost speak over each other as if oblivious to what the other is saying.

Personnel: **A**
           B

A: It is of supreme importance

B: that we get our image of Jesus

A&B: RIGHT.

A: For there are too many blithering idiots,

B: well-meaning people,

A: religious schismatics,

B: church leaders,

A: Marxists,

B: Tories,

A: anarchists,

B: establishment figures,

A&B: WHO ARE LEADING PEOPLE ASTRAY.

A: So, listen carefully …
          Jesus,

B: — as we all know,

A: came from a model family

B: — his mother was pregnant when she got married.

A: And lived in a secure home

B: — they were refugees.

A: As the old hymn says,
'Throughout his wondrous childhood' …

B: — about which we know next to nothing …

A: 'he was mild and obedient' …

B: — he did a bunk when he was twelve.

A: Jesus was the model working man,

B: — he became redundant when he was thirty,

A: encouraging entrepreneurship in others

B: — he told Peter, Andrew, James, John,
Matthew to give up their jobs.

A: He kept good company,

B: — dining out with beggars and prostitutes.

A: He had a good word for everybody,

B: — 'vipers', 'blind guides', 'hypocrites'.

A: His conversation was about the finer things in life,

B: — dough, sheep, pig farming, wise virgins …

A: He never dabbled with controversy

B: — he just claimed to be the Son of God!

A: Jesus never upset anyone by his language

B: – except priests, pharisees, pigeon sellers, executioners and wealthy young men.

A: He was respected in religious circles

B: – they wanted to lynch him after his first sermon.

A: Jesus was a man among men

B: – and women.

A: He was a man of God

B: – he was the Son of God.

A: In his majesty we see God at work

B: – in his humility we meet God in person.

A: That's why he was worshipped

B: – that's why he was crucified.

A: Jesus isn't here now

B: – he rose again on the third day.

A: So we have to get on with it ourselves

B: – he sent his Holy Spirit to guide us.

A: We have to build the kingdom!

B: – we have to celebrate his presence among us.

A: We have to give a lead!!

B: – we are to follow where he calls …

A: stand up and be counted …

B: – humbly …

A: like soldiers!!!

B: – as servants.

A: We are a mighty army.

B: We are the body of Christ.

A: It is of supreme importance

B: that we get our image of Jesus

A&B: RIGHT.

Power

This poem may be read by two voices, changing mid-verse. A setting 'The Keel Row' is available in the HEAVEN SHALL NOT WAIT collection.

Power stalks the earth both by purpose and accident,
filling with pride those it does not fill with fear.
Power may be hidden or power may be evident,
macro or micro, far off or very near.
> Look to the one who has chosen to live without
> power to seduce or corrupt or to repel;
> learn from the one who refuses to scream and shout,
> yet can convince that with him all will be well.

Power of computers to file information may
keep for the few what the many should be told.
Power of the party which governs the nation can
seldom be challenged and rarely be cajoled.
> Look to the one who embraces the frightened folk,
> those more aware of their wrong than of their right;
> learn from the one who will speak for the silenced ones,
> hear for the deaf, and provide the blind with sight.

Power of the privileged in talent or parentage
discounts whoever it cannot understand.
Power of the bureaucrat, anxious at every stage,
struggles to keep what's unstructured close at hand.
> Look to the one who forgoes his advantages,
> sits on the ground with whoever cannot stand;
> learn from the one who has known our predicament,
> baffled all systems, and lived from mouth to hand.

Power of the press on the button or media
kindles the fuse to a scandal or a bomb;
power of the keeper of secret or confidence
puzzles what purpose to use the secret for.
> Look to the one who speaks peace unpretentiously,
> defuses hate and is antidote for fears;
> learn from the one who accepts, unconditionally,
> those whom he summons to share his joy and tears.

That we worship one God

Affirmation 1

Leader: That we worship one God,
Creator, Christ and Holy Spirit,
in whose image we are made,
to whose service we are summoned,
by whose energy we are renewed:

ALL: THIS WE BELIEVE.

Leader: That it is central to the mission of Christ
to respect the earth as God's possession,
to rejoice in the diversity of human culture,
to preserve human life in all its beauty and frailty,
to witness to the love of God for all people and all places
and to invite others to share that converting experience:

ALL: THIS WE BELIEVE.

Leader: That through the power of the Holy Spirit
the persecuted shall be lifted up
and the wicked shall stumble,
the hesitant prayers and hidden actions of God's people
shall change the course of human history,
the ancient words of scripture
shall startle us with fresh insight:

ALL: THIS WE BELIEVE.

Leader: That God has called the church into being
to be the servant of the kingdom,
to be a sign of God's new order,
to offer a foretaste on earth
of the magnificence of heaven:

ALL: THIS WE BELIEVE.

Leader: That Christ, fully aware of our differences,
prays that we may be one
so that the world might believe:

ALL: THIS WE BELIEVE
AND TO THIS WE ARE COMMITTED
FOR THE LOVE OF GOD
IN THE WAY OF CHRIST
BY THE POWER OF THE HOLY SPIRIT.

The big wave
Script 3

This is best read slowly and in darkness, with readers using torches or candle-light and plenty of snoring and clamour.

Ref: Mk.4:35–41

Personnel: **Narrator**
                Jesus
                A, *a disciple*
                B, *a disciple*
                C, *a disciple*

Narrator: He was sleeping,

Jesus: *(Snores)*

Narrator: … sleeping in the bow of the boat,
the sleep of a child …
the sleep of a happy child …

A: Jesus, did you see that wave?

Jesus: *(Snores)*

Narrator: He was sleeping,

Jesus: *(Snores)*

Narrator: and nothing disturbed him …
not the wind …
not the weather …

B: Jesus, this is getting rough!

C: Jesus, this is getting really rough!

A: Jesus, did you see that wave?

Jesus: (Snores)

Narrator: The sound of the sea ...
the sound of the pounding ...
the break of the waves ...
the creak of the boat ...

B: Jesus, I'm scared!

C: Jesus, I'm terrified!

A: Jesus, I'm going to spew (be sick)!!!

Jesus: (Snores)

Narrator: I will keep him,
keep him in perfect peace
whose mind is set on me ...
waking or sleeping ...
waking or sleeping ...

B: Jesus, can you swim?

C: Jesus, we're sinking!

A: Jesus, do something!

A,B,C: (Together, confused and ad lib)

Waken up! Jesus, Jesus! Come on! Help us!

Jesus: (Loudly) Shshshsh ...

(Quieter) Shshshsh ...

(Sternly) ... Oh where's your faith?
... even your little faith?

In the storm, in the darkness,
I am with you.

Let the waves roar,
but don't be distressed.

Otherwise you may never hear me saying,
'Peace!
Be Still.'

The Cana of Galilee case

If the script is read in a church, good use can be made of the pulpit as a witness box and the lectern as the desk for the prosecution. The Lawyer should dress in black or in a black gown, Domino appears like a small-time businessman and McGuinness is a wilting French waiter.

Four candles in wine bottles should be placed prominently and lit, preferably not far from the witness box.

Ref: Jn.2:1–10

Personnel: **Lawyer**
             Peter Domino, *a licensed trader*
             Moshe Ben McGuinness, *a wine waiter*
             Voice off

Lawyer: Call Peter Domino.

Voice off: Peter Domino!

                 (Domino comes to the witness box)

Lawyer: Are you Peter Domino,
                 licensed trader in wines and spirits
                 who frequently features
                 in television and newspaper advertisements
                 holding a French poodle with a blue rinse?

Domino: That is correct.

Lawyer: Do you swear?

Domino: Sometimes.

Lawyer: In that case,
                 we'll dispense with the oath.

Mr Domino,
you wish to raise an injunction
against the Cana of Galilee Arms Hotel,
Cana Road, Galilee,
in pursuit of your allegation
that the said establishment
has wilfully flouted the Trades Description Act.
(Or similar local legislation)

Could you tell the court, Mr Domino,
what has compelled you
to take this action?

Domino: Everybody's buying Meldorado.

Lawyer: Could you elaborate, Mr Domino?
What is 'Meldorado'?

Domino: Meldorado is a rich tawny wine.

Lawyer: A wine of good quality, Mr Domino?

Domino: Certainly not!
It tastes like a cross
between aftershave and furniture polish.

Lawyer: And why has there been a sudden rush to buy it?

Domino: Because of what happened
in the Cana of Galilee Arms.

Lawyer: Could you explain a little further, please?

Domino: The Cana of Galilee Arms is,
as you have heard,
on the Cana Road, Galilee.
My wine store is three hundred yards away
on the Poodle Parlour side.

Last week,
we were asked to supply six crates of Meldorado
for a wedding reception …
which we did.

I'm not exactly sure what happened,
except that all the MD …
I mean, Meldorado …
was quickly tanned …
or finished …
and the empty bottles were returned to the cellar.

I am informed
that some twenty minutes later,
the same bottles were returned to the tables,
replenished with a nectar
which, in my humble opinion,
could only have been
some very rare Chateau Neuf du Liebfraumilch
Pape Entre Deux Mers Beaujolais … 24 BC.

Accordingly,
news of the 'new look' Meldorado
spread like wildfire throughout the neighbourhood.

By evening there were queues of donkeys and carts
parked nose to rear outside my shop
while the owners fought with each other
to secure our limited reserves of Meldorado.

But by closing time,
the same donkeys and carts had returned
with the unsatisfied customers
breathing all kinds of malicious threats.

They claimed to have been swindled.
Meldorado was Meldorado,
as it was, is, and ever shall be.

Lawyer: Is it your fault, Mr Domino,
that the wine failed to satisfy?

Domino: Not at all!
The fault does not lie with my retail outlet.
The fault lies with the Cana of Galilee Arms
which has obviously flouted the Trades Description Act
by substituting for Meldorado
a vintage vastly superior.

Lawyer: Have you anything else
you'd like to say, Mr Domino?

Domino: No, but I'd quite like to burp.

Lawyer: Then the quicker you leave the witness box,
the better.

(Domino leaves)

Call Moshe Ben McGuinness.

Voice off: Moshe Ben McGuinness!

(McGuinness makes his way to the witness box)

Lawyer: Are you Moshe Ben McGuinness,
Chief Steward and Wine Waiter
at the Cana of Galilee Arms Hotel?

McGuinness: I am.

Lawyer: Were you stewarding
at the wedding reception last Thursday
for which Peter Domino,
Licensed Trader in Wines and Spirits,
supplied six crates of worst quality Meldorado?

McGuinness: I was.

Lawyer: Do you know
how the empty Meldorado bottles were replenished
with Chateau Neuf du Liebfraumilch
Pape Entre Deux Mers Beaujolais 24 BC?

McGuinness: Non!

(Pause)

But I do know
how the empty Meldorado bottles were replenished
with Prix D'Excellence Marquis de Sauterne Caves
Hirondelle Sangria D'Anjou *25* BC.

Lawyer: Please tell the court how this happened …

McGuinness: A carpenter's son told the waiters
to fill the empty bottles with cold water.

Lawyer: And did they?

McGuinness: Mais oui.

Lawyer: Why?

McGuinness: Because they thought
he was going to play a tune on them.

Lawyer: And did he?

McGuinness: Mais non.

He said something,
je ne sais quoi,
and he told the waiters
to return the bottles to the tables.

When the people drank –
quelle surprise!

Lawyer: Do you mean to say
that water drawn from an artesian well
in your back court
has suddenly taken on alcoholic propensities?

McGuinness: I do not know.

Lawyer: Do you recognise any of the bottles in the court?

McGuinness: Mais oui.

(Pointing)

That is them over there.

Lawyer: And are these alcoholic candles
burning in them by any chance?

McGuinness: Mais non.

Lawyer: Then why are they there?

McGuinness: Just to remind us
of how a very ordinary person
took some very ordinary drink
among very ordinary people
and enabled them all to be happy.

Lawyer: Have you anything else to say?

McGuinness: Non ...
but just wait
until he gets his hands on bread and fishes!

The family
Reading 4

Occasionally our material arises from situations where there seems to be no appropriate text available for the theme of a meeting. This was the case for this poem. A monthly event, Last Night Out (which the Wild Goose Worship Group enabled), wanted to reflect on the Fifth Commandment, about honouring parents. Preparatory Bible study indicated how, for Jesus, family was neither nuclear nor extended, but a unit of belonging based on commitment to him rather than genetics or biology.

The poem can also be sung. The music is found in the collection LOVE & ANGER.

He had no wife, no family,
he had no children of his own;
he once had been a refugee,
despised but never left alone.
To all the widowed and the fatherless
he showed the love that none had shown.

He liked to watch as children played
and knew the lyrics of their song;
he cared for those that lived at risk,
the ones whose rights had all gone wrong.
The plight of helpless and homeless folk
would always in his heart belong.

He had no job to pay the rent,
but women gave him house and food;
they saw in him no hidden threat,
his singleness was safe and good.
And those whom no one ever listened to
discovered that he understood.

He chose to eat in simple style
beside the wounded, hurt and poor;
he told them tales to make them laugh
and, for their stigma, was the cure.
In crowds and circles of rejected folk
his generosity was sure.

Those whom he calls his family
are this through love and not reward:
sisters and brothers we can be,
if we but take him at his word.
And so we join to celebrate the life
of Jesus Christ, our friend and Lord.

The song of the crowd
Reading 5

This text may be read or sung to the folk tune 'Kingsfold', as contained in the HEAVEN SHALL NOT WAIT collection.

Ref: Mk.6:35–44

To him who walks among the crowds
let's show our gratitude:
we came to him a hungry mob,
and his response was food.
This is the teacher well renowned
for talk of sin forgiven.
Some prize his smile, some pull his robe,
some say he comes from heaven.

Who are you, lean-faced traveller,
whose words surpass all law,
whose past was spent in industry
with hammer, nails and saw?
Who are you, time-served carpenter,
now that you've changed your trade
to hosting casual lakeside feasts
with food you never made?

But why the silent modesty,
and why the shaking head?
You're worth a thousand bakers
for you multiply the bread!
We'll make you king and gladly sing
songs to re-tell your story.
So why not stay? Why move away?
Do you refuse our glory?

There goes the man whose eyes can scan
a crowd and tell their need.
There goes the one whose words we shun
when keen to frown or feed.
He walks from here while people peer
at his all-knowing face
which speaks of how each one who stares
has, in his heart, a place.

The wedding
Reading 6

This monologue should be read, ideally, by a woman in her fifties who looks the antithesis of the pale, wan and fragile stereotypes of Mary. When John's Gospel opens, Jesus is thirty years of age. His mother is therefore no longer a naive teenager (if she ever were). The monologue has to have a sense of gregariousness in it as Mary – witnessed to in scripture – seems to dare her son to redeem a wilting wedding feast.

Ref: Jn.2:1–10

He was thirty when it happened.

There was no warning;
he had never done that kind of thing before,
though we had been at plenty of weddings.

But this was a really big wedding.
It was Isaac Morgenthaler's daughter
who was marrying a boy from the city
and everyone in our village was invited.

So I says to him
'Listen, Jesus,
there's going to be a lot of nice girls at this affair.
You're 30 and you're not getting any younger.
So don't be backwards at coming forward
just because your old mother's there.
I'll not be watching you.'

Well he just rolled his eyes the way his father used to,
so I said no more.

At any rate,
we got to the wedding
and into the reception
and what a spread …

There was breaded octopus,
roast quail in pomegranate sauce,
pickled locusts
… and mushroom omelettes for the vegetarians.

Everything was magnificent …
except for the olives.

Now personally I don't like olives
– they talk back to me –
but everyone who ate them said they were very salty.

So between that and the heat
– it was about 32°C (*87°F*) –
there was a lot of drinking going on.

We must have been sitting at the table for over two hours,
everyone was talking at the top of their voice.
And then I noticed it got distinctly quieter, maudlin even.

So I turned to our Jesus and I says,
'I think that's the wine run out.'

He just turned to me, rolled his eyes and said,
'Your powers of observation are beyond me, mother.'

But I knew from the way he said it
that he might be up to something;
so when I saw him rising from the table
and going into the kitchen,
I said to one of the waiters,
'You see that man walking towards the kitchen,
that's my boy.
Follow him and do what he tells you.'

Well, exactly what happened after that I don't know.
There are about a dozen different stories.

According to Jesus,
he just asked
for the big wine jars to be filled with water.
Then he lifted them one at a time,
gave them to the waiters
and told them to take them to the tables.

Well, in no time at all, the noise level was at its peak
and everybody was congratulating Mr Morgenthaler
on the beaujolais nouveau.

When Jesus came back to the table,
I said to him,
'Jesus, how come with all the water jugs in my kitchen
 you've never turned your hand to the wine-making before?'

He just rolled his eyes the way father used to
and then he said,
'Mother,
 I just wanted everybody to be as happy
 at this wedding with wine,
 as you are in your kitchen without it.'

Well, that was all in the past,
but ever since
there's been a constant flow of invitations
from people who would like Jesus to come to their wedding.

Told not to tell
Script 5

As the script progresses, Peter should become peripheral, as if he is interrupting a conversation between the two brothers.

Ref: Matt. 17:1–9

Personnel: **Peter**
James
John

Peter: *(to James)* So …

James: So …

(Pause)

Peter: *(to John)* So …

John: So …   *(Pause)*

Peter: So, am I the only one with a tongue in my head?

James: He said we weren't to talk about it.

John: No, he said that we weren't to tell anybody else about it until …
you know … 'later'.

Peter: So …

(Pause)

Peter: So what did you think?

John: I thought you made an absolute fool of yourself.

Peter: I might have known you would say that!

John: Oh, come on, Peter!

James and I were just standing, gawking,
trying to take it all in,
and you're running about like a headless chicken
gathering wee (*little*) bits of rock.

Peter: I was trying to build cairns ... one for each of them.

John: Not bad, Peter!
We are just being offered a private viewing
of the three greatest people in history,
and you think it's time for elementary architecture!

(Pause)

James: Which one was Moses?

John: The one with the stammer.

James: How do you know he had a stammer?
We were standing about twenty yards away.

John: I was watching his lips.

James: Any other distinguishing features?

John: Yes, he didn't have any shoes on.

James: Oh, *that* was Moses.
So the other one must have been Elijah ...
He looked quite old to me.

John: He's been dead about six hundred years.

Peter: John, that's irreverent!

John: Peter, at least I looked at them.
You were building a rockery, remember.

Peter: It was a cairn.

James: But what did you think about Jesus?

John: What did you think?

James: I've never seen him in white before.

John: White? It hurt my eyes!

James: *(Excitedly)*
It was like when my mother used to bleach the sheets,
and hang them out to dry on the graveyard wall.
Remember that John?

John: James, it was worse than that …
I mean, it was better than that …
It was … magnificent!

Peter: So, what are we going to tell the others?

John: Do you mean about your architectural endeavours?

Peter: No … about the whole thing.

James: I thought we had established
that we weren't to say a word
until after he has … been … 'raised'.

Peter: That's right.
But what will we say then?

John: We'll just have to invent a term
that nobody will want to ask about.

James: What about a word that sounds like a medical condition?

John: Yes … or a serious operation.

(Short pause)

Peter: What about …
What about 'transfiguration'?

Who am I?
Reading 7

This text may be read or sung. The music is available in the ENEMY OF APATHY collection.

Ref: Jn.14:6

Who am I?
Not the one you choose.
Who am I?
Not the one you lose.
Who am I? I'm the one
from whom you grew away
until you heard what seemed absurd –
I am the Way.

Who am I?
I'm the one you tend
in those whose lives
might break or mend.
My hands, unknown, you've held,
my people's pain you've quelled;
their gloom dispelled, you heard me say,
'I am the Way.'

Who am I?
I'm the course of years,
the force of life,
the source of tears:
the laughter in the room,
the talking in the street
is where we meet. These too convey,
I am the Way.

Who am I
when regret or fear
demands you wonder
why you're here?
I'm not the instant answer
to your quick request.
You should have read, I only said,
'I am the Way.'

Who are you?
Not the one you were
before you learned
to love and care.
Who are you?
You're the one
with whom I want to share
my faith, my food, my cross of wood,
my will, my way.

With God all things are possible
Meditation 4

During this meditation each section may be ended either with a short (i.e. four-bar) musical interlude or by the assembly singing the chant WITH GOD ALL THINGS ARE POSSIBLE.

Ref: Jn.1:10

Personnel: **A**
           B
           C
           D
           E

A: He was in the world,
but the world,
though it owed its being to him,
did not know him.
He came to his own,
but his own would not receive him.

But to all who did receive him,
to these who gave him their allegiance,
he gave the right to become children of God.

So the Word became flesh,
and lived …
among …
us.

ALL: *(Short musical interlude or sung response – see opposite)*
WITH GOD ALL THINGS ARE POSSIBLE,
ALL THINGS ARE POSSIBLE WITH GOD.

With God, all things are poss - i - ble; all things are

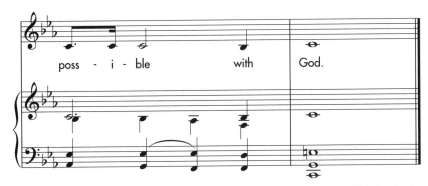

poss - i - ble with God.

B: He took five loaves and two fish
and blessed and broke them
and fed a crowd.
And no one understood,
but all forgot their hunger.

He spat on clay to moisten it
and rubbed the mixture on the eyes of a blind man.
And no one understood,
but the man began to see.

He lay asleep in the midst of a storm
and when wakened,
told the winds and waves to be quiet.
And no one understood,
but all became calm again.

ALL: *(Short musical interlude or sung response)*

C: He was in the line of the prophets.
He was able to meet with the great.
He knew people of knowledge and intellect.

But when it came to showing
who was greatest in the kingdom of heaven,
he did not take a ruler
or a wise man
or a guru.

He put a child in their midst
and said, 'Unless you become like a child,
you'll never enter the kingdom of heaven.'

ALL: *(Short musical interlude or sung response)*

D: He called people to follow him,
to leave self behind and to go with him,
to take up their cross
and to keep in step
with him who carries the weight of the world.

'Whoever cares for her own safety is lost,' he said.

'Whoever loves husband, wife, parent or child
more than me is not worthy of me,' he said.

'Whoever loses himself for my sake,
will find his true self,' he said.

ALL: *(Short musical interlude or sung response, followed by a pause)*

A: He came to his own,
but his own would not receive him.
Yet to those who do receive him,
to those who give him their allegiance,
he gives the right
to become sons and daughters of the living God.

64

You are the unseen guest

Prayer 3

Leader: You are the unseen guest at every table;
you are the unknown goal to which all strive;
you are the unnamed source of inspiration;
you are the untamed grace on which we thrive;
you are our Saviour,
ALL: WE ARE YOUR PEOPLE.

Leader: Welling up in the song of children,
willing laughter in a friendly room,
crossing paths coincidentally,
smiling in the face of doom,
you are our Saviour,
ALL: WE ARE YOUR PEOPLE.

Leader: Taking time to weave tomorrow,
taking care to mend today,
taking thought where we were thoughtless,
noting what we meant to pray,
you are our Saviour,
ALL: WE ARE YOUR PEOPLE.

Leader: For this, our gratitude.
for you, our yes.
ALL: AMEN.

The company of Jesus

Among the women Jesus met
Script 6

Here we are introduced to some of the lesser-known women in Jesus' ministry. They should take their seats near each other and in front of the assembly. These should be choir rather than lounge seats, to avoid the script looking like a chat show. A few bars of music may back up the dialogue as indicated.

Ref: Lk.8:3 (Susanna); Matt.26:6–13, Mk.14:3–9 (the woman who anointed Jesus); Mk.1:29–31, Matt.8:14–15, Lk.4:38–39 (Peter's mother-in-law); Matt.20:20–28 (James and John's mother)

Personnel: **Narrator**
        Susanna, *a disciple*
        Samantha, *the woman who washes Jesus' feet*
        Betty, *mother-in-law of Simon Peter*
        Mrs Zeb, *mother of James and John*

Narrator: Among the women Jesus met were …
        the widow of Nain whose son had died,
        the Canaanite woman whose daughter was ill,
        the crippled woman he saw in the synagogue,
        Joanna, the wife of Chuza,
        and a woman called Susanna.

        (Susanna takes her seat)

        Among the women Jesus met were …
        Jairus' daughter,
        Mary of Magdala,
        a woman who covered his head with ointment,
        a whore who washed his feet with her tears.

        (Samantha takes her seat)

        Among the women Jesus met were …
        Martha and Mary who lived in Bethany,
        Mary and Martha, the sisters of Lazarus,
        a woman who haemorrhaged for over twelve years
        and the mother-in-law of Simon Peter.

(Betty takes her seat)

Among the women Jesus met were …
a Samaritan with at least five husbands,
Mary the mother of James and John,
Salome who witnessed the crucifixion,
and Zebedee's wife who was proud of her sons.

(Mrs Zeb takes her seat)

Among the women Jesus met were …

Susanna: Susanna.

Samantha: Samantha.

Betty: Betty.

Mrs Zeb: Hyacinth.

(Music)

Susanna: I used to be married,
but it didn't work out.

Like Joanna, my friend,
I married a civil servant
and ended up with an uncivil husband,
working for a corrupt regime.

In some ways it suited me …
there were the receptions,
the parties, the privileges.

But there were also the poor,
the homeless,
the disposable people
whom my husband despised,
yet to whom my conscience directed me.

I had to break out.
I was fed up being his possession
to be displayed rather than a wife to be loved.

I had a small private income.
So I left him.

Samantha: You can call me whatever you like.
It doesn't bother me now.
I was all these things, and more.

But I was never cheap.
No. I've always had style …
scarlet satin dresses,
fox furs in the winter,
bangles, baubles and beads,
and the occasional cigarette in a long holder.

I won't say I was happy.
It was not my choice to be a floozie,
but if your husband dumps you
and you have no means of support,
and you're an orphan
with no family to fall back on,
what can a girl do?

I did what I had to …
and most of the time I hated it
and hated myself.

But there was nothing else for it.
I had to live,
and if I was going to be a whore,
I was going to do it in style.

Betty: Betty's the name …
Betty to my friends,
Elizabeth to my in-laws
(they were very posh),
Mum to Sandra, my daughter
and I'm never sure what Peter calls me.
He's Sandra's husband.

I didn't want them to get married.
I didn't like him much.
He looked scruffy and he had a terrible accent.

I said to our Sandra,
'He's a fisherman.
They stink.
You'll never get the smell out of the washing.
If you put his shirt in with your sheets,
you'll end up lying on winkles and starfish.
You mark my word.'

But she wouldn't listen.

I said,
'Why not go after a banker, Sandra …
 or an accountant.
They don't smell.'

But it was no use.

Still, he was good to me when Jack died.
They took me in,
gave me a room
and Peter got me to mind his stall in the market
on Tuesdays and Fridays.

Mrs Zeb: We're in business.
'Zebedee and Sons' is the title,
though I, the dear wife and mother,
do most of the work.

My husband inherited the business from his father
and, strictly speaking,
it should be passed on to James and John.
But that's very much under debate at the moment.

I've always been proud of my children.
I think mothers should be.
I've pushed them forward when they needed it …
and boys always need a prod!

And I've been keen
that they always kept good company …
I expect them to bring all their friends home.
I want to see them.
I don't want them mixing with anyone beneath them.
We have our reputation to preserve.

Narrator: These … Susanna,
                Samantha,
                Betty,
                Hyacinth,
these were among the women who met …
Jesus.

(Music)

Susanna: I was really apprehensive about him.

He wasn't from my class or background,
but there was something
of sincerity in him …
no, not so much sincerity as integrity.
He was real.

And when he spoke,
underneath I knew
that what he said was true.

And when he spoke to me,
it was because of who I was,
not because of whose wife I was …
or had been.

I felt that he valued my opinion,
and learned from my experience.

So when Joanna suggested
that we should help to finance him,
I drew out money from the bank,
and gave it to Judas.

I offered my house when they needed it, and …
along with other women …
I followed him.

Samantha: I never thought that I would do it …
you know …
wiping his feet with my hair and all that …
but I did.

The reason I came to know about him
was because of a jibe
some boy shouted at me one night …
'Why don't you go and see Jesus.
They say he likes girls like you.'

It was shouted in derision,
but I took it seriously.

Men had always come looking for me,
but I had never gone looking for a man.

I watched him twice when he was speaking.
There was no threat in him
to people whose life had gone off the rails.

There was a lot of hope in him.
There was a lot of forgiving in him.
And that's what I needed …
forgiving.

And that's why I broke into a rich man's party
and washed his feet with my tears.

I knew he would let me be sorry
and I knew he could make me whole.

Betty: I never liked him much,
to tell you the truth.
I had no idea who he was,
and I wasn't religious.
So I didn't want to know.

But I was appalled
when Peter started going after him.

I said to him,
'Listen Peter,
you've got our Sandra to look after,
and if she hasn't told you I will:
she's five months gone!

You've got responsibilities …
family responsibilities,
and you've got the boat to attend to
and the market stall.

You can't go wandering round the countryside
after a carpenter.'

But he wouldn't listen.

Mrs Zeb: I was more than pleased
when I heard that James and John
had attached themselves to Jesus.
I was very proud.

A substantial number of people in the community …
influential people …
had said to me privately
that they believed he was the genuine article.

Not being an expert in Jewish Messiahs,
I had nothing to compare him with,
though I must say
his appearance left a little to be desired.

The boys told me
that he had called them
from mending the nets.

They were uncertain
as to whether to go or not.
So I took them.

I said to myself,
'They'll be glad of this one day.'

And whenever they came home,
I'd ask them to remember me to him
the next time they saw him.

(Music)

Narrator: Among the women Jesus met
were Susanna, who supported him,
Samantha, who washed his feet,
Betty, Peter's mother-in-law,
and the wife of Zebedee …

And, having met him,
they were changed.

Disciples of Christ
Meditation 5

As this dialogue is read, small candles may be brought from different parts of the worship space to be placed round a cross on a table or a chair in the centre. The text should be read slowly with music played underneath to enable the movement. There may then follow a prayer thanking God for faithful women – or a conversation about why we remember the twelve male disciples more than the females. Alternatively, it may be followed by the meditation YOU WILL NOT ALWAYS HAVE ME (Page 155).

Ref: Lk.1:46–55 (Mary); Lk.1:5–25, 39–45 (Elizabeth); Lk.2:36–38 (Anna); Lk.10:38–42 (Martha); Lk.8:3 (Joanna); Mk.1:29–31, Matt.8:14–15, Lk.4:38–39 (Peter's mother-in-law); Jn.4:1–41 (the Samaritan woman); Matt.15:21–28 (the Canaanite woman); Matt.9:20–22, Mk.5:25–34, Lk.8:43–48 (the haemorrhaging woman); Mk.12:41–44, Lk.21:1–4 (the poor widow); Jn.8:1–11 (the woman caught in adultery); Matt.26:6–13, Mk.14:3–9 (the woman who anointed Jesus)

Personnel: **A**
             B

A: Let us remember
and celebrate twelve of Jesus' disciples,
people who were touched by and who tended him.

B: Remember Mary,
the girl from the country town,
the poet and singer,
who became pregnant with God,
by God, for God's sake.

A: Remember Elizabeth,
Mary's older cousin,
who shared Mary's excitement,
who herself bore John,
the friend and baptiser of Jesus.

B: Remember Anna,
the old widow and faithful believer
who saw an eight-day-old baby
and recognised that the Messiah had come.

A: Remember Martha,
the cook and housekeeper,
the plain speaker,
who gave Jesus her anger
so that he could give her his love.

B: Remember Joanna,
who with Susanna and many other women,
provided the hospitality
which Jesus saw as crucial to the Gospel.

A: Remember Peter's mother-in-law,
who was so grateful to be healed
that her first act after recovery
was to make a meal for Jesus.

B: Remember the Samaritan woman
whose conversation with Jesus
was full of double entendres,
but whose life was so changed by him
that she became the first real evangelist.

A: Remember the Canaanite woman,
who gave Jesus a hard time,
taking his exclusive language to task,
until he saw and admired
her toughness and devotion.

B: Remember the haemorrhaging woman
who contaminated countless men
in her struggle to touch Jesus,
who named her faith as the root of her cure.

A: Remember the poor widowed woman,
who, in giving the smallest coins to God,
gave Jesus his model for generosity.

B: Remember the woman caught in adultery,
who let Jesus show
how the grace of God is greater
than the moralising of men.

A: Remember her
whose perfume filled a room with fragrance,
yet who let her costliest gift
be offered, in love, to God.

I sang for him
Meditation 6

This meditation consists of four monologues which can be used individually or may be spoken by the four women in sequence. When the latter is done, it is best to have the assembly sing after each. A verse from the following is suggested, although songs appropriate to the congregation may be used.

Four individual sung responses may be:
  1. JESUS LOVES ME (v.1),
  2. IT'S ME, O LORD,
  3. NOBODY KNOWS THE TROUBLE I'VE SEEN,
  4. OVER MY HEAD, I HEAR MUSIC IN THE AIR.

A sung response suitable for all is DEO GRATIAS (from THERE IS ONE AMONG US).

Ref: Matt. 19:13–15, Mk. 10:13–16, Lk. 18:15–17 (the child Jesus blessed); Jn. 11:1–44 (Mary); Lk. 1:46–55 (Mary, Jesus' mother)

Personnel: **Woman 1**, *the child Jesus blessed*
          Woman 2, *Mary, sister of Martha and Lazarus*
          Woman 3, *Mary, Jesus' mother*
          Woman 4, *Salome, a disciple*

Woman 1:   I sang for him,
          but I can't remember it all.
          I was only three, according to my mother.

          I was always inquisitive,
          but never as much as on the day
          when I wandered through the legs
          of a crowd of old men
          and ended up in the middle of a circle.

          He stopped talking to the men
          and he said to me,
          'What's your name?'

'Jennifer,' I said.

'Jennifer?' said he,
'I don't think I've ever met a wee (*little*) girl
called Jennifer.

'Come on and stand beside me
and take a look at these nice men.'

So I went over to his side,
and I looked at the men,
but they didn't look very nice;
they looked annoyed.
So did my mother.
I could see her at the back.
I could see her saying,
'Wait till I get my hands on you, lady.'

Then he put *his* hands on me
and said to all the old men,
'You've got to become like this wee (*little*) one
to get into the Kingdom.'

And then he said to me,
'Can you sing, Jennifer?'

I nodded my head.
So he said, 'On you go, just for me.'

And I sang …
just for him,
and he said 'God bless you, Jennifer.'

ALL: *(Sung response)*

Woman 2:   I sang for him,
the day after my brother died.

I had gone to get him.
I wanted him to come,
just to be there,
just to let Martha and me talk,
                            cry,
                            feel we were understood.

79

He had already heard the news.
And that made it difficult to know
why he wouldn't come,
why he was staying in the same place.

I was at my wits' end.

I asked him, 'What can I do?
                What is there to do?'
and he said,
'Sing ...
but don't sing a happy song.
Sing of how you feel and where you are, Mary.
Let God hear the trouble in your soul.'

So I sang.

I sang, 'How long, O Lord?'

I sang, 'God, why have you turned your back?'

I sang, 'Lord, don't be deaf to my cry.'

I sang all the old psalms that never get sung.

And he listened.
And when I couldn't sing, for tears,
he kept the song going.

And now and again,
he'd hold my hand and give it a squeeze
and say, 'God bless you, Mary.'

ALL: *(Sung response)*

Woman 3:   I sang for him,
and I think he knew it
even if he couldn't hear it.

I don't know
how the words came
or where they came from.

Pregnant women have funny cravings,
but I never thought mine would run to poetry
or song writing.

But I sang it,
for him in the womb
and for God who had put him there.

And I sang with conviction,
because I knew that one day
he would bring down the mighty from their thrones
he would lift up the lowly,
he would fill the hungry with good things,
he would turn the rich away empty-handed.

And when he grew up,
I saw him do all these things,
and I saw him take the consequences.

When they buried him,
and when I was alone again,
the words came back to me.

I hadn't sung them for years,
and I don't know where I found the strength
to sing them then.

But I did.

I did it because I believed,
despite everything,
that there would be another day
when I'd sing the words in his company
and he'd say as he often did,
'Bless you, mother.'

ALL: *(Sung response)*

Woman 4:   I sang for him,
because I couldn't believe my eyes.

I had heard the rumour.
I had been to the graveyard.
I had seen Peter running through the streets
looking haunted and delirious at the same time.

But I didn't believe it.
I mean, how could I?

And then, I saw him.

I was mending Joses's shirt,
although my mind wasn't on the mending.
I just kept thinking,
'Is it true? Or is it just a story?'

At any rate,
I was mending Joses's shirt,
and I was humming away
at a tune we were all fond of.

And after a while I broke into the words,
'Oh give thanks to the Lord
 for his love endures for ever' …
that's the women's line …
at least it is the way we sing it.

I had no sooner sung 'endures for ever'
when I heard somebody answer with the men's line:
'Oh give thanks to the Lord,
 for the Lord alone is good.'

I looked up,
my mouth fell open
and my darning fell on the ground.

He just looked at me with the biggest smile
and said,
'God bless you, Salome.'

ALL: *(Sung response)*

If you were busier, Lord

Prayer 4

Leader: Let us pray.

If you were busier, Lord,
you would not bother with us.
But you have time for all;
you have time to listen.

ALL: SO WE PRAISE YOU,
FOR HAVING ALL THINGS IN PROPORTION,
AND A TIME IN YOUR SILENCE
FOR US TO SPEAK.

Leader: If you were wiser, Lord,
you would not bother with us.
But you are foolish
and thus we are your choice.

ALL: SO WE PRAISE YOU
THAT YOUR KINGDOM IS INDEED UPSIDE DOWN;
THAT YOUR STANDARDS
ARE NOT THE WORLD'S STANDARDS;
THAT YOU HAVE BENT DOWN TO TOUCH US.

Leader: If you were content, Lord,
you would not bother with us.
But you are restless.
Through anger,
through excitement,
and through love,
you will all things to change
and be made new.

ALL: SO WE PRAISE YOU,
THAT YOUR RESTLESSNESS HAS BEEN BORN IN US
AS THE PAIN OF THE WORLD,
THE CRIES OF YOUR PEOPLE,
THE URGENCY OF YOUR GOSPEL,
AND YOUR HOLY SPIRIT
UPSET OUR EASINESS
AND REQUIRE US TO RESPOND.

Leader: With the eye of a weaver,
you have chosen us –
such different threads –
to be gathered into unity
that the world might believe.

ALL: SO MAY WE NOT SERVE YOUR PURPOSE
UNLESS WE ARE OPEN TO EACH OTHER;
NOT CARE FOR EACH OTHER
UNLESS WE REFLECT YOUR LOVE;
NOR DARE TO LOVE LIKE YOU
UNLESS WE ARE GLAD TO ACCEPT
THE COST AND JOY OF DISCIPLESHIP,
AS FRIENDS AND FOLLOWERS OF JESUS
IN WHOSE NAME WE PRAY.
AMEN.

Look at your hands

Closing responses 1

Leader: Look at your hands.
See the touch and the tenderness.
ALL: GOD'S OWN FOR THE WORLD.

Leader: Look at your feet.
See the path and the direction.
ALL: GOD'S OWN FOR THE WORLD.

Leader: Look at your heart.
See the fire and the love.
ALL: GOD'S OWN FOR THE WORLD.

Leader: Look at the cross.
See God's son and our Saviour.
ALL: GOD'S OWN FOR THE WORLD.

Leader: This is God's world
ALL: AND WE WILL SERVE GOD IN IT.

Leader: May God bless you.
May God keep you ever with great care
and lead your lives with love.
ALL: MAY CHRIST'S WARM WELCOME SHINE IN OUR LIVES,
AND PEACE IN HEART AND HOME
PREVAIL THROUGH EVERY DAY
TILL GREATER LIFE SHALL CALL.
AMEN.

Lord Jesus, when you took a child

Prayer 5

Ref: Matt.18:1–5, Mk.9:33–37, Lk.9:46–48

Lord Jesus, when you took a child
and told adults to become like her
if they wanted to enter your kingdom,
what did you mean?

Are we to be naive or to ask questions?
     To be innocent or to be trusting?
     To be shy or to sing?
     To be docile or to be open-eyed?

Show us how to become
not the ideal child we imagine
but the real child you blessed.

Teach us,
if we have done too much growing up,
how to grow down.
AMEN.

Polly Androus revisited
Script 7

This reflection is in two parts, the first of which is simply a verbatim retelling of the biblical story. A song (an ALLELUIA) or a silence might precede and follow the reading. The second half of the script, which is an interpretation of how the characters felt in the course of their interaction, may then be used.

Ref: Jn.4:1–41

Personnel: **Jesus**
Polly, *the woman at the well*
Reader

(A song or silence)

Jesus: Excuse me …

Polly: Yes?

Jesus: Could you give me a drink?

Polly: You are a Jew.
I'm a Samaritan.
We don't drink from the same cups.

Jesus: If only you knew what God gives
and who it is
that is asking you for a drink
you would ask him
and he'd give you life-giving water.

Polly: Sir …
you haven't got a bucket
and the well is deep.

Where would you get that life-giving water?

It was our ancestor Jacob
who gave us this well;
he and his sons and his flocks
all drank from it.

You don't claim to be greater than Jacob,
do you?

Jesus: Whoever drinks *this* water
will be thirsty again;
but whoever drinks the water
that I will give her
will never be thirsty again.

The water that I give
will become in her a spring
which will provide life-giving water
and give her eternal life.

Polly: Sir, give me that water:
Then I'll never be thirsty again,
nor will I have to come here to draw water.

Jesus: Go and call your husband and come back.

Polly: I ... I haven't got a husband.

Jesus: You're right
when you say you haven't got a husband.
You've been married to five men,
and the man you live with now
isn't really your husband.

You've told me the truth.

Polly: Sir, I see that you are a prophet.
My ancestors worshipped God on this mountain.
They were Samaritans,
but you Jews say that Jerusalem is the place
where we should worship God.

Jesus: Believe me,
the time will come
when people will not worship the Father
either on this mountain or in Jerusalem.

You Samaritans don't really know
whom you worship,
but we Jews know whom we worship
because it is from the Jews
that salvation comes.

But let me tell you,
the time is coming …
indeed it's already here …
when by the power of God's Spirit
people will worship the Father as he really is,
offering him the true worship that he wants.

God is Spirit,
and only by the power of his Spirit
can people worship him as he really is.

Polly: I know that the Messiah will come,
and when he comes,
he will tell us everything.

Jesus: I am he …
I who am talking with you now.

(A song or silence)

Reader: Jesus, travelling to Galilee,
came through the region called Samaria.

He came to a well
which had first belonged to Jacob,
and he sat down there.

It was about noon,
and he was tired out travelling.

A Samaritan woman …

Polly: That's me,
in case you're interested …

Reader: A Samaritan woman came to draw some water.

Polly: Actually I was just curious.

Nobody ever draws water in the middle of the day.
It's too hot.

In fact, I was about to have a siesta,
when I just happened
to see a dusky stranger enter my territory.

Reader: Jesus said to her,

Jesus: Give me a drink of water.

Polly: Are my ears deceiving me,
or did I hear you …
a Jew,
asking me …
a Samaritan …
for a wee (*light*) refreshment?

Well, I had to say that …
Jews never eat or drink with us.
They're scared they'll get infected.

So, I thought to myself …
any Jew who asks for a drink,
is wanting more than a drink.

Jesus: If only you knew what God gives,
and who is asking you for a drink,
you would ask him,
and he would give you life-giving water.

Polly: I took one look at him,
and thought I had landed myself with a nutter (*madman*).

The one minute he's asking for a drink,
the next he's getting all religious,
and then he says
he could give me 'life-giving' water.

What was he going to hold it in … his shirt?

So I says,
'Where's your bucket, big boy?

This is a deep well, you know.
It was one of our famous ancestors,
a man called Jacob,
who gave us it.

You're not trying to make out
that you're better than him, are you?'

Jesus: Whoever drinks this water
will be thirsty again.
But whoever drinks the water I give,
will never be thirsty again.

Polly: Oh, I'll have some of your stuff, then …

Just once on my lips
and then satisfied for ever.

Added to which …
I'd stop getting bow-legged
carrying buckets and pails
up and down the stairs
night and morning.

Fair exchange …
you have some of mine,
and I'll have some of yours.

Jesus: Go and call your man.

Polly   Well....
when he said that,
my heart just leapt.

This was him just trying to find out
if I was 'available'.

So I knew what to say.

Jesus: Go and call your man.

Polly: (Innocently)
Eh …
I don't have a 'man'.

Jesus: You're dead right,
             you don't have a man.
             You've had five
             and that's not including your present 'bidie-in' (*lover*).

Polly: Well, I just about passed out.
             Here's me
             working up to a passionate embrace,
             and it turns out I'm talking to the C.I.D. (*F.B.I.*)

             'You must be a prophet!' says I.

Prayers that Jesus hears

Meditation 7

Two reading desks are required for this script – one for the Leader and one for the others. Either the Bridget KYRIE shown or the Ghanaian one (from the MANY & GREAT collection) may be sung by a choir and/or the congregation. The script can lead into prayers with the assembly being invited to light candles. If this is the case, an appropriate area should be set aside and the sung response KINDLE A FLAME (from the HEAVEN SHALL NOT WAIT collection) be sung.

Ref: Lk.18:13 (The taxman); Jn.11:28–37 (Martha); Matt.8:1–4 (The leper); Jn.20:11–18 (Mary)

Personnel: **Leader**
Taxman
Mary, sister of Martha
Leper
Mary M, Mary Magdalene

Leader: This is a prayer which Jesus heard,

'Lord, have mercy on me ... a sinner.'

Taxman: *(Pause)*
I was never good with words,
except when it came
to furthering my own interests.

And I had furthered my own interests,
in the way that people do
who know how to make money
by fair means and foul.

And then I got fed up with self-interest.
It did not make me happier.
It made me greedier and more callous,
more like the men I had detested
in my idealistic youth.

That's when I went into the House of God,
ready with a rehearsed speech
to appease heaven and soften up my Maker.

But I never made the speech.

When I got there,
I realised that God's love was greater
than the anger I imagined he had for me.

I broke down
and blurted out:

Lord, have mercy on me ... a sinner.

Lord, have mercy on me ... a sinner.

(Pause)

God hears that kind of prayer.

ALL: *(Sung response, KYRIE ELEISON)*

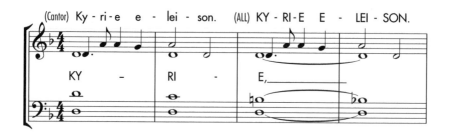

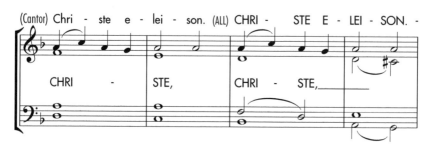

Leader: This is a prayer which Jesus heard,

'Lord, if you had been here …
it wouldn't have happened.'

Mary: *(Pause)*
They told me to restrain myself.

They told me that if I saw him,
I shouldn't make out that he was to blame.

They said,
'Your sister Martha has already told him
how you're feeling.'

So, I put on a calm face –
well, as calm as you can
three days after your brother has died.

I ran out to the main road to meet him.

Then, suddenly, my composure went.
I put my arms round him
and clung to him in love and anger.

I said,
'Lord, if you had been here …
it wouldn't have happened.'

'Lord, if you had been here …
it wouldn't have happened.'

(Pause)

God hears that kind of prayer.

ALL: *(Sung response, KYRIE)*

Leader: This is a prayer which Jesus heard,
'Lord, if you want to …
   you can make me better.'

Leper: I was not a hopeless case.

I could still walk;
I could still hold things in my hands;
I could still speak.

I was horrible to look at …
I know that
because nobody looked at me.
It was as if one quick glance
was enough to set them muttering
'there but for the grace of God …'

But I knew it was getting worse.
It was only a matter of time before …

Well, at any rate,
where I got the courage from,
I don't know.

Nobody pushed me.
Indeed some folk jumped out the way
when they saw me coming.

He just stood still …
not rigid …
but still.

He looked at me
as if he had been waiting for me,
as if he really wanted to hear me say,

'Lord, if you want to …
you can make me better.'

'Lord, if you want to …
you can make me better.'

God hears that kind of prayer.

ALL: *(Sung response, KYRIE)*

Leader: This is a prayer which Jesus heard,
'Sir … if you took him away,
 tell me where you have put him.'

Mary M: It all seems a bit silly now,
but it wasn't then.

I had lost people before …
my mother,
then my father
when I was in my teens.

I lost a brother at sea
and a best friend through cancer.

But I didn't think I would ever lose Jesus.

I was sure of him;
I was close to him;
I knew his interest in me
his love for me.
This was all real.

I had faith in him.
It was real too.

And then it stopped.
The voice was silent.
The body was gone.
And my memories were haunted
by hellish laughter …

No Jesus …
no faith …
no future ….

Do you blame me,
if with my head down
and my eyes fixed meaninglessly on the ground,
I didn't know who I was speaking to
when I said,

'Sir … if you took him away …
tell me where you have put him.'

'Sir … if you took him away …
tell me where you have put him.'

(Pause)

God hears that kind of prayer.

ALL: *(Sung response, KYRIE)*

Leader: So, if we want to make a prayer
for forgiveness
or of frustration,
for healing
or of searching faith,
for ourselves
or on behalf of one other person,
let us do that now.

And if lighting a candle helps
to focus our prayer,
we can do so as we sing.

ALL: *(Sung response, KINDLE A FLAME)*

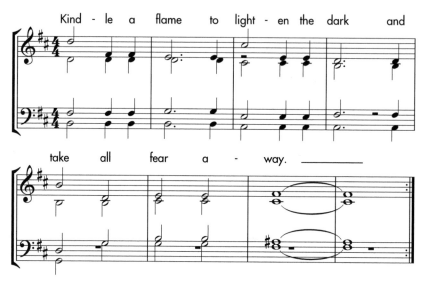

Racist or redeemer?
Script 8

For best effect, this script should be read with the Reader, Jesus and the Woman facing the assembly. They speak as if oblivious to each other, offering their own interpretations of the incident. The Host and James can stand at the side or behind the assembly.

Ref: Matt.l5:21–28, Mk.7:24–30

Personnel: **Narrator**
Jesus
Woman, *the Syro-Phoenician woman*
Host
James

Narrator: Jesus went away to the countryside
near the city of Tyre.

Jesus: I went into a house
to get away from the crowds.
I didn't want anyone to know I was there;
but it was impossible.
I couldn't stay hidden.

Narrator: A woman who was a Gentile
heard where Jesus was.

Woman: 'Gentile' is a posh word for foreigner,
and 'foreigner' is a posh word for heathen.

I came from Syria.
No self-respecting Jew would have entertained me.
They called people like me scabs,
or scum,
or parasites,
or words I could never repeat here.

Host: She's telling the truth.

I'm a Jew
and I learned all these names for 'foreigners'.

It was my house Jesus was staying in.
You can imagine how I felt
when *she* came to the door.

But when she told me her story,
I felt sorry for her.
So I let her in.

Woman: I didn't go for me;
it was for my wee lassie (*little girl*).
Something had got into her.
I don't know what.
She was going off her head.
It was as if she was possessed or something.

Narrator: When the woman saw Jesus she called out,

Woman: Have mercy on me, Son of David.

(Then addressing the assembly in a different tone)

I gave him his proper title,
so that nobody could say
I wasn't minding my manners …

Jesus: I wasn't pleased to hear her.

I had given strict instructions
that I wasn't to be disturbed.
I was tired and needed a rest.

I asked why she had been let in.

Host: And I said
that it was my house and my decision.

Narrator: Then she fell at Jesus' feet
and begged him to heal her daughter.

Jesus didn't say a word to her,
but his disciples came
and begged him to send her away,
because she had been following them
and making a terrible noise.

James: Well so she had.
She had been going on like a lunatic,
and I could feel my face going all red
with embarrassment.

I mean, she didn't belong to us;
she was a heathen.
We had to remember our reputations.

Narrator: Then the woman cried out,

Woman: Please help me, sir!

Host: This was all happening in my living room.
It was the first time
I'd ever had the likes of her in my house.

I don't know what ever possessed me
to let her in in the first place.

Narrator: Jesus said,

Jesus: Let us feed the children first.

James: I was glad to hear him say that.
After all,
we're the children of Israel,
and some of us were hungry,

Host: … and I was hoping
he might do his trick
with the loaves and fishes again.

Jesus: Let us feed the children first.
It isn't right to take the children's food
and throw it to the dogs.

James: When I heard that
I wanted to shout Hurray!

Host: When I heard that I said to myself,
'Thank God.'

Woman: When I heard that my heart sank …
dogs …
bitches …
tinkers …
It was just what you'd expect a Jew to say!

Jesus: That's why I said it.
It was just what a Jew would be expected to say.
It's just the kind of racist thing
that James or John might come away with.

I saw them smirking.
I saw the man who owned the house
looking relieved.

What they didn't see
but what the woman saw
was the wink in my eye.

Woman: Just in the nick of time
I realised that he was having me on.

He was using the kind of language
the others wanted to hear.

So I played along with him
when I saw the twinkle in his eye.

He had said that it wasn't right
to throw the children's food to the dogs.

So I looked at him all coyly and said,
'But Jesus,
 the dogs under the table
 eat the children's scraps.'

Host: 'Cheeky midden (*upstart*),' I thought,
and I was about to show her the door
when I noticed that Jesus was smiling.

James: I was going to give her a mouthful,
but I saw that Jesus wasn't annoyed.

It was as if he had fed her the punch line
and she had delivered it on cue.

Jesus: It was clear as the light of day to me.
This woman was a good woman,
and she was a tough woman,
and she wanted the best for her daughter.

Her being a Gentile couldn't change that.
I admired her for bursting into a house
full of Jews,
and I was moved by her faith.

So I told her …
and all the others …
how much I admired her.

And then I said,
'What you want will be done for you.'

Narrator: That's the precise moment
when the woman's daughter recovered.

Host: And it's the precise moment
when I realised that Jesus was the Redeemer,
and not the racist I wanted him to be.

Save us, Lord, from the temptation

Prayer 6

Save us, Lord,
from the temptation to buy what we do not need;
from confusing what we need with what we want;
from wasting what we do not own,
from owning what we will never use;
from idealising the past as a golden age;
from bequeathing our children a sorry inheritance.

Strengthen the arm and the will of all who,
for the good of the world you made and love,
challenge our greed
and inform us about appropriate living.

May their words gain a good hearing
so that the world may have a good future.
AMEN.

Somebody special
Meditation 8

This meditation can be used at the end of a busy day at a conference or retreat. It was originally written for use at a festival. It will therefore be necessary to substitute appropriate allusions, landmarks or locations. At the end, a sung response, such as O LORD, HEAR MY PRAYER (from Taizé), may be used.

It's about 8 o'clock.
The light is beginning to dim
and you are beginning to wilt.

It has been a long day,
a busy day,
a noisy day …
so many people speaking, singing,
so many messages being given
by speakers in every room.

Looking for a bit of peace,
you walk away from the biggest conference room,
and come to a smaller circular room
which looks as if it might be empty.

'I'll go in here and get my head together,'
you think.

You walk round until you find the door
and as you walk in,
you just hear the last syllable of a word
when all hell seems to be let loose.

Lying on their backs on the floor
are forty or fifty children
between seven and ten years of age.

Round the walls are some women …
probably mothers.

Music is blaring and a rainbow ball
is being thrown up in the air
from one child to another.

Whoever the ball descends on
sends it spinning back up in the air
to land on someone else, somewhere else.

And the children shout and cheer,
especially when the ball makes to land on them.

Then the music stops,
and the child on whom the ball drops
holds on to it.

And, from the side,
a man makes his way
towards the child holding the ball.

The man is tall, thin,
wears narrow green canvas trousers,
a white shirt and a baggy brown cardigan
which seems to drop from his shoulders
almost to the ground.

He has light golden hair,
is slightly balding,
and has a pointed nose and rimless glasses.

He goes over to the child,
a little girl,
and while she holds the ball,
he puts his hand on her head and says:

'You are Denise
and you are somebody special
because God gave you freckles,
so that if the sun doesn't shine,
all you have to do is smile and the world
will be a warm place.'

She smiles ...
the world does become warm,
the children all cheer,

back on goes the music again,
and the ball is thrown up in the air.

After a minute or so,
the music stops again
and the man goes over to a boy
who is grasping the ball tightly.

He kneels down,
puts his hand on the boy's head
and all the other children listen intently
as he says:

'You are Rhavind,
 and you are someone special,
 because God needed a brown friend
 for all the white boys and girls here …
 and he chose you to be that friend.'

Rhavind smiles bashfully,
the children cheer,
and a boy lying next to Rhavind
puts his hand on Rhavind's shoulder
to show that they are friends.

On goes the music,
up goes the ball
and a minute later,
when the music stops,
the ball is being clasped by a little girl
who has a very large hearing aid in each ear.

The man comes over,
kneels beside her,
puts his hand on her head
and she watches his lips intently as he says:

'You are Pamela,
 and you are somebody special,
 because you can speak with your hands
 and you are going to give everyone this message.'

Then he says something silently,
which she lip reads.

She then stands up in the middle
and the other children sit up to watch.

With great simplicity and confidence,
Pamela makes signs which can only mean:

'It's time for bed.
 Let's pick up our clothes
 and go back to our parents.'

Some of the children make a complaining noise,
but in the end
all of them cheer.

They gather up their belongings,
and many of them,
before they go out the door with their mothers,
go over to the man –
one at a time –
and whisper something in his ear.

When all have gone,
you go over to him
and sit on a bench beside him.

'You've a great way with children,' you say.

'I like children,' he replies.

'Tell me, do you know *all* their names?'

He almost blushes …

'Yes … *all* of them …
and they're all special.
Each one is a somebody.'

'What was it they whispered to you at the end?' you ask.

'I wouldn't tell a soul,' he says and then …

'In any case,
 you don't need to hear what the children say.
 You've got a lot to say yourself.

This has been a busy day for you ...
confusing ...
loud ...

You came into this room
because you wanted to find somewhere quiet ...

You wanted to spend some time on your own ...
to find God maybe ...
in order to complain,
to ask something,
to make sense of what confuses you,
to remember somebody you don't want to forget.

Well ...'

And here he puts his hand on your head.

'Well ...'

And here he calls you by name.

'Well ...'

God has found you.

So let the conversation begin.

(Pause)

Let us talk to God,
in our own way,
of the things that matter
at the end of this day.

(Silence, followed by a sung response)

Steal, Jesus, steal
Prayer 7

Steal, Jesus, steal from us
> the grudge we will not let go
> the pain we will not let heal
> the sin we most condemn in others ...
>> and most disguise in ourselves

Liberate, Jesus, liberate in us
> the hands that care for only one body,
> the eyes that focus on what they want to see,
> the tongues that condemn the petty,
>> but never challenge the powerful.

Join, Jesus, join in us
> the frayed ends of broker temper,
> the notion of conviction to the practice of commitment,
> the tip of our fingers to the hem of your garment.

Love, Jesus, love in us
> the self we despair about,
> the self we hide,
> the self we throw at others
>> because we cannot live with it on our own.

And when you have stolen the sin from us,
> liberated our potentials,
> mended our brokenness
> and love our withered selves,
give us the grace to do for others
what you have done for us.
AMEN.

↑ Testimony and prayer of three anonymous children

Symbolic action 1

This, as its title suggests, is both a reflection and a prayer.

The readers represent three anonymous children whom Jesus met. They read as adults reflecting on the experience of their childhood, and asking to be like children again.

If this material is going to lead in to prayer – which it can do very easily – every worshipper should have in his or her hand three individual pictures which can be photocopies of the illustrations shown below. Please note, it is important that they have three separate pieces of paper and not one A4 sheet with three diagrams. Some cutting up is required.

The leader of worship should indicate that, for this meditation, two things are required: firstly that we sing before and after its three sections; and secondly that we look at one picture at a time beginning with (1). A suitable song might be YOUR KINGDOM COME, O LORD (from the MANY & GREAT collection).

It may be helpful for the leader of worship to say that, as the meditation proceeds, there may be children known to the worshippers who come to mind. If so, they might like to write names down on the reverse of the appropriate picture.

There should be a cross in the centre of the worship area. If prayer is to follow on from the meditation, let there be a short silence. Then the worship leader should suggest that if particular children have been brought to mind whose plight or potential people would like to lay before Jesus, they may do so, as the song resumes, by placing the appropriate picture – with or without a name on the back – around the cross. After the activity, the worship leader might say a short prayer offering the action of the worshippers to God.

Ref: Jn.6:1–13; Lk.8:40–41 & 49–56; Matt.19:13–15

Personnel: **A**, *the boy with the loaves and fishes*
B, *Jairus' daughter*
C, *the child of whom Jesus said, 'Suffer the little children'*

ALL: *(Sung response)*

A: When I was a child,
I gave him all I had.

He stood among hungry people
who needed fed.
And I believed that he knew
how to make the food go round.

Now that I am an adult,
I have much more to share.
But, though the crowds are still hungry,
I am reluctant to give him what I have.

Lord, when today I see the faces
of those who long for food and justice,
when I hear their cry,
make me as generous as when I was a child.

ALL: *(Sung response)*

B: When I was a child,
he told me to get up.

Outside my window,
the neighbours were saying,
'She's a hopeless case.
There's no help for her.'
But he put them to silence
and told me to get up.

Now that I am an adult,
sometimes doubt, sometimes frustration,
sometimes failure, sometimes sadness
surround my bed;
and I hear the voices
of those who criticise
more easily than I hear
the voice of the one who encourages.

Lord, when I hear the voices outside which condemn
and the voices inside which discourage,
make me as keen to listen to you
as when I was a child.

ALL: *(Sung response)*

C: When I was a child,
he put his hand on me.

Others wanted to keep me away,
believing he had better things to do.
But I pushed my way through the crowd,
and sat on his knee and let him embrace me.

Now that I am an adult,
sometimes I think that he is too busy
and often I say that I am too busy
to let his hand rest on me.

Lord, when so many excuses keep us apart
make me as keen to let you embrace me
as when I was a child.

ALL: *(Sung response)*

The calling of Peter
Reading 8

This monologue may be read, by an older woman, on its own or in association with the Gospel reading about the call of the disciples.

Ref: Mk.1:29–31, Matt.8:14–15, Lk.4:38–39

Mother-in-law: I'm sorry I mentioned my pension.
You'll all be thinking,
'She must have a penny or two.'
But I don't actually.

I have my own house –
that's where Peter used to live.
When he married my daughter Sandra,
he moved in with us.

I get some money from a baker's shop
which my nephew took over
when my husband died,
and that's what keeps Sandra
and the two boys while Peter's away.

I remember when he went.
I saw exactly what happened.

Somebody said
that there was a preacher on the beach.
So I went down with Jason ...
that's Sandra's second child ...
he was eleven months old ...
at the teething stage ...
Sandra needed a break,
and I thought I'd like to hear the preacher.

So I went and sat and listened,
and he was very good ...
he talked a lot of sense.

Actually he said some quite unusual things …
he talked about
how the kingdom of God was here on earth;
he said that it was breaking in as he spoke,
and that all the people who were last
were going to be first,
and all the people who were never listened to
were going to be heard.

I could see
that some of the older men found that hard to take,
especially when one of the younger women said,
'That's us he's talking about, girls!'

Well, after he had finished,
I saw him walk over
to where Peter and Andrew were standing.
They were repairing their nets.

And I began to walk over,
because I thought
I'd quite like him to bless the baby.

He just looked both of them straight in the face
and said,
'Follow me.
I need you to help me to catch people.'

And the pair of them dropped what they were doing
and walked off.

I shouted to Peter,
but he wouldn't listen.
He just said, 'Tell Sandra I won't be long, nan.'

That was three years ago.

Now, to be fair,
he does come back quite a lot.
And he does a bit of fishing when he's at home,
but he'll only be here three days at the most
and then he goes away to help Jesus.

People ask me why he went.
They think
that this 'Jesus' must have put a spell on him.

They even suggest
that he's glad to be away
from his nagging old mother-in-law.

But it's not that.

I think Jesus saw something in our Peter
that Peter never knew was there.

I think Peter realised that Jesus understood him
even though he had never met him.

And when somebody who knows you
through and through says,
'Follow me,'
maybe you have to go.

The identikit
Script 9

The Detective is interviewing two women about a personality they claim to know. The Detective has a dry sense of humour. A is quite matter of fact, B a bit of a gossip, who likes playing second fiddle and runs her lines into those of A. NB: This script only works in areas where 'aye' is the common term for 'yes'.

Other material of a similar nature and with a Christmas theme can be found in the CLOTH FOR THE CRADLE collection.

Personnel: **Detective**
A
B

Detective: So, you say you saw her.

A: Well, not exactly 'saw',
but we know plenty who did.

B: Plenty, aye.

Detective: So, what was she like?

A: She'd be about 28 or 29.

B: 29 if she was a day.

A: She was about 5'2" or 5'3" tall.

B: 5'3" at the very most.

A: And she had a pale complexion,
… very white.

B: She could have been taken for a corpse.

A: And she was thin … very thin.
In fact, maybe even anorexic.

B: Anorexic, aye.

Detective: And how was she dressed?

A: In blue.

B: Blue, aye …

Detective: Just one blue eye, was it?

(Puzzled looks)

A: She had a blue thing over her head.

Detective: A balaclava, perhaps?

B: *(Dead serious)*
No, it was too big for a balaclava.
It was more like a shawl.

A: Hanging down.

B: Hanging down, aye.

A: And she had a long blue dress,
in fact, it was more like a cloak,
… just like a nun.

B: Like Mother Teresa herself, God rest her soul.

Detective: Mother Teresa died in her nineties.

A: *(Indignant)*
She was like Mother Teresa in her early thirties.

B: Thirties, aye.

Detective: Did you hear her speak?
Did she have an accent?

A: She was very quiet.

B: Quiet, aye.

Detective: She didn't have a noisy eye?

(Puzzled silence)

A: She never spoke up.

B: She wouldn't say boo to a goose.

A: Very soft spoken.

B: You could hardly hear her.

A: But she had a cultured accent.

B: Quite posh actually.

A: But quiet.

B: Quiet, aye.

Detective: Anything else?
Anything else you know or noticed?

A: She kept herself composed.

B: Composed, aye … like Beethoven.

A: She could sit still for ages.

B: She could hear the grass growing.

A: Very placid nature.

B: Placid, aye.

Detective: What about a name?

A: I don't know,
but I imagine it would be something like …
Zephyrella …

B: Or maybe Lorentia

A: Or Carminaria.

B: ... aye, or maybe even Emphysima.

Detective: So, she's small, 28
                dressed in blue from top to toe,
                politely spoken,
                placid
                and called by some exotic name.

A: That's her, sergeant.

B: That's the very wumman (*woman*).

Detective: It may be the very woman,
                but it's not who we're looking for.

A: Who's that then?

Detective: She's about sixteen and a half,
                5'10",
                athletic,
                wears jeans,
                stripey pullovers and Doc Martins,
                weighs about 10 stone,
                helps out in a joiner's shop,
                sings in a folk group
                and looks eight months pregnant.

A: And what's her name, sergeant?

Detective: Mary.

A: Oh, that couldn't possibly be her.

B: No, it couldn't be her.

The royal party
Script 10

This is a good script to use at an all-age service in church as well as in a less formal atmosphere. It involves a group of people, who least suspect it, being invited to come forward and share in the royal party. This should not be children only, but a cross-section of those present.

It is really the Herald, rather than the King (or Queen) who holds the action together. The Herald has to have proven powers of ad-libbing, particularly when he wanders among the audience trying to discern who would be good to bring to the party. While being a lively character, he must watch not to overdo his part.

The King should be dressed with a robe and crown, the Herald with some kind of uniform or livery and the three principal guests as befits their occupations. The only prop required is a gift-wrapped box of sweets. A musician (pianist or fiddler) should be at hand to provide music for pass the parcel, failing which the Herald could operate a record or cassette player. In either case, the music maker must have a good view of the game, and particularly of the King.

The three principal guests should have seats in different places throughout the audience. They could either process there during appropriate music, or they could be seated in advance and surprise the audience by speaking in bold and expansive tones.

The King should be in a central position – perhaps in the pulpit or behind a lectern, but able to come to a raised platform area for the game. The Herald should be outside the main area or hidden in a balcony or at the back of the audience, suddenly springing to life when his cue word is mentioned.

Note that the sex of the character can often be changed to suit the players. Oliver can become Olivia and Stephen Gary can become Stephanie Gloria.

At the end of the script a suitable song, such as LORD OF THE DANCE, should be sung by the congregation as the party-goers return to their seats.

Ref: Lk.15:15–24

Personnel: **Lady Lucy Pewcy**, *a fashion model*
Stephen Gary Swift, *a racing driver*
Oliver Forsythe-Slime, *a self-made business man*
The King (or Queen), *a genial, absent-minded kind of monarch*
The Herald, *a lively character*

Pewcy: *(She stands)*
I am Lady Lucy Pewcy.

I model clothes for these and those
and such as those.
When I go out to visit,
I dress and look exquisite.

Lady Pewcy ... Lady Lucy Pewcy.

Swift: *(He stands)*
I am Stephen Gary Swift.

I drive an MG racing car
and I'll go far
because I feel
like a million dollars behind the wheel.

Stephen Gary Swift –
one day I might give you a lift.

Slime: *(He stands)*
I am Oliver Forsythe-Slime.

I'm a very important businessman,
though I started my life with a grocer's van.
Now I'm the owner of 26 stores,
each one with six or seven floors.

Oliver Forsythe-Slime –
I'm always doing overtime.

(They all sit)

King: *(Stands and addresses everyone in a friendly way)*
I am the King (*or Queen*),
and I'm a silly old thing (*or bean*).

I'm not very good at poetry ...
so I'll just speak normal.

When you're the King,
you can do what you like.
And because I am the King I could do what I like ...

I could cut off the heads of people
who don't laugh at my jokes.

I could decide that the country
was going to be run by children.

I could make a law
so that every boy and girl had to go to bed
every night at half past five.

I could order everyone
to drink a bottle of cod liver oil every day.

But I'm not like that.
I don't want to terrify my people.
I want to love my people.

So ... I think ...
I think I'll have ... a party.

Herald: *(Appearing from nowhere)*
A party? A party?
Did I hear someone mention a party?

King: Yes, I did.

Herald: *(Bowing)* Oh ... Your Majesty.

King:... But who are you?

Herald: I'm the Herald.

King: Are you the Royal Herald?

Herald: *(Shaking his head)*
No, I'm the Glasgow Herald *(or appropriate local name)*.

King: The Glasgow Herald ... good.

Then why don't you go to Glasgow *(or appropriate locality)*
and ask people there to come to my party?

Herald: But who will I ask, your Majesty?

King: Ask the people who are important in Glasgow.
(Or appropriate locality)

Herald: Very good, sir.

(He leaves the king who sits to the side. The Herald hums or whistles an appropriate tune as he/she journeys to the centre of the audience)

Now ... I wonder who I should ask?

(Here he/she ad libs as he/she moves through the audience, stopping at random people)

Would you like to go to the King's party?

Oh, wait a minute ...
I smell a funny smell ...
Would it be your feet?

(Other ad libs the same way)

You look tired ...
you would fall asleep.

You've got a dirty neck ...
I don't think you've washed today.
You couldn't come like that.

You don't look as if you could dance all night.
You wouldn't be much good.

(After three or four rejections, Lady Pewcy coughs and stands. The Herald moves towards her)

Herald: Why ... It's Lady Pewcy ...
Lady *Lucy* Pewcy ...
and if I might add, Ma'am,
you're looking rather juicy.

(She feigns modesty)

Would you like to come to the King's party?

Pewcy: Would I like to come to the King's party?
Why, of course I would.

But whatever would I wear?

(She muses)
Should I come in furs?
Or would a gold lamé dress
be the order of the day?
Or what about
a cunning little fishnet and leather number?

But if it's the King …
I really should have diamonds.

(To the Herald)

When is this party?

Herald: Just now, Ma'am.

Pewcy: You mean right now?

But I couldn't come dressed like this.
Why, I look like a laundry basket!

I'm sorry …
If it's now …
I haven't got time to change.

Herald: As you wish, Ma'am.

(Pewcy sits. The Herald goes round other people until Swift coughs and stands. The Herald moves towards him.)

Herald: Gary Stephen Swift?

Swift: Stephen Gary Swift, actually.

Herald: Of course.
Would you like to come to a party?

Swift: Who's holding it?

Herald: The King.

Swift: The King?
Well, I'm just going
to inspect the new Lancia I've bought.
I wanted to make sure
that it has an automatic hairdryer installed.
Very important.
When is the party?

Herald: Now.

Swift: Now?
But I've got to go and see my new car.

Herald: But Stephen Gary ... it's the King!

Swift: Listen, sunshine ...
tell his Majesty thank you very much,
but I must have that automatic hairdryer.
And I must make sure it's installed in the car today.

Herald: As you wish.

(Swift sits. The Herald moves on and approaches Slime)

Oliver Forsythe-Slime ... am I right?

Slime: *(He stands)*
You're right.
Let's talk business.
You want to sell me your corner shop?
I'll give you £50,000.
No more, no less.

Herald: I don't want to sell you a shop.
I want to invite you to a party.

Slime: I'm too busy!

Herald: But it's the King who's sending out the invitations.

Slime: I don't believe in Kings.
And I'm too busy anyway.

And if you don't want to sell me your corner store,
stop wasting my time and your vocal cords!

(He sits down immediately)

Herald: Well what now?

(He goes towards some children looking as if he'll invite them, then changes his mind and makes for the King)

Your Majesty ...!

King: *(Rising)*
Yes ... are they all coming?

Herald: Eh ...
nobody wants to come to the party.

King: Nobody?
Who did you ask?

Herald: I asked all the important people ...
people like Lady Lucy Pewcy, the fashion expert,
Stephen Gary Swift, the sports car driver,
Oliver Forsythe-Slime, the big businessman.

King: And they didn't want to come?

Herald: No ... they said they had other things to do.

King: So all the important people have no time for the King?
Well, their King will now let them know
that he has no time for them.

I'll let the world see who are my real friends.

When you were doing your rounds,
did you see anyone who had smelly feet,
or a dirty neck,
or who couldn't dance?

Herald: Yes ... lots.

King: Then go and invite them to my party.

Herald: But, your Majesty!

King: Go and invite them to my party ...
on you go!

(The Herald goes back into the audience and gathers a band of outsiders. These he/she brings them up to the King and gets them to sit or stand in a circle)

Herald: That's them all,
but you still have room for more.

King: Then go back to the town and find some more.

Don't look in the obvious places.
Look for the people who don't have a job or a title …
or who seem too old, or too young …
people who don't have anything wrong with them …
people who are just ordinary.

I want them to come.
I want my house to be full.

Herald: As you wish, sir.

(As the Herald goes back to get others, the King welcomes his guests and gets them to sit down)

That's everyone here, your Majesty.

King: Good … and you're all welcome.

And because this is a party …
I think we should have a game.

But I'm not very good at games.
I'm not very good at poetry,
and I'm not very good at games.

Herald, do you know a party game?

Herald: What about Postman's Knock?

King: The Royal Mail doesn't deliver on a Friday evening!
(Or other evening or Sunday morning)

Let me think …

Oh, I know … Pass the Parcel.

(The King goes and picks up a hidden parcel)

I have a parcel here which hasn't been opened yet.
Why don't you pass that?
Herald … you organise it.

(The Herald takes the parcel and gives instructions)

Herald: I'll give the parcel to someone
and they pass it to the next person on the left,
and they pass it to the person on their left.
And when the music stops,
the person who has the parcel opens it up.

Now for some music!

*(Meanwhile the king gets into the middle among the kids who
are passing the parcel. Music starts and the parcel is passed
until it reaches the King and then the music stops.)*

Herald: Oh! This is a fix!

King: No … the music stopped with me …
So I'll open the parcel.

(He opens it and inside is a jar/box of sweets)

Well … I could keep these all to myself …
but I won't.

I invite to my party people who don't feel important,
and people who feel left out.

I want to share with them
all the good things that I have,
and I want them to share these good things with each other.

So everyone will get a sweet.
But first let's have a song.

*(Sweets are given out and people return to their seats during
a song)*

There is one among us
Meditation 9

This reading is particularly appropriate during Lent, as the characters featured appear in the Lenten stories. Each character should read with an inflection of annoyance, envy or joy as the text suggests. After each voice, it is appropriate to sing the response THERE IS ONE AMONG US.

Ref: Mk.5:21–42, Lk.8:40–56 (Jairus' daughter); Lk.8:1–3 (Joanna); Matt.26:6–13, Mk.14:3–9 (Simon); Lk.10:38–42 (Martha)

Personnel: **A**, a male neighbour of Jairus
             B, a female friend of Joanna
             C, a male acquaintance of Simon
             D, Martha, sister of Mary and Lazarus

A: He was holding her hand,
            and it was in her bedroom,
            and he was thirty-three,
            and she was twelve.

            Does he have to court scandal?
            Or is it –
            to use the 'in' phrase –
            that he was 'touch-hungry'?

            A different thing an hour before
            when a woman old enough to be his mother
            made a grab for him.

            Oh, he wasn't for that.
            He was for none of that.
            He likes them young, obviously.

            I know her father.
            I spoke to him.
            I said,
            'Jairus, I'm surprised at you,
            letting this kind of behaviour
            happen in your own house
            with your own daughter.'

He never said a thing.

It seems there's a conspiracy of silence
about the matter.

ALL: *(Sung response)*

THERE IS ONE AMONG US
WHOM WE DO NOT KNOW;
HOST OF HIGHEST HEAVEN,
PRESENT HERE BELOW.

B: I said to her,
'Joanna, you're off your head.
How many times is that he's stayed with you?'

She wouldn't be drawn.

So I said,
'They'll have lice the lot of them.
You don't know where he and the other two slept
before you gave them the spare room.'

'Do they pay you?' I asked her,
'I mean do they ever bring you anything …
a salmon,
or some wild honey
or flowers even?'

But she wouldn't be drawn.

So I said,
'What does Chad think about it?
Or is he never at home
when you 'entertain' them?
Or does he not know what you're doing;
in his home with his money?'

But she wouldn't be drawn.

(Sung response)

C: I was a bit shocked
when I heard the guest list.

Shocked …
and peeved (*annoyed*),
to be honest.

I always thought
that I was one of Simon's friends,
but obviously wealth was the criterion.
There were four merchant bankers,
five head accountants,
two people who worked in exports,
a professor of business management,
and a handful
of what you might call 'senior rotarians'.

But the shock was not that I was excluded.
The shock was who was the guest of honour.

Reputedly he is on the side of the 'poor',
a kind of social democrat I suppose.
Allegedly he is quite critical of financiers,
though I hardly imagine
he'll have the first clue about economic growth.

So why this champion
of the proletariat *(or common man)* was there …
laughing …
and drinking wine …
and eating venison …
I don't know.

I know that some people
will do anything to get votes,
but it isn't as if there's an election.

Venison … that's what they had.
Moira told me.

(Sung response)

D: I thought at first he was giving me a row.

I went all petted *(all awkward)*,
my lip quavering for fear I had offended him.

And then he broke into this big smile
and started imitating me
drying dishes and pouring tea.

He's a very good mimic,
but then he's been in my kitchen often enough
to see what goes on.

'Martha, Martha,' he said,
'… Martha, Martha.'

So I took off my apron
and I tied it round his neck.

'Jesus, Jesus,' I said,
'… Jesus, Jesus.'

… and the pair of us giggled like children.

(Sung response)

They were sitting on the ground
Reading 9

After this reading about Jesus' transforming ministry, which some opposed, it is
appropriate to sing a song celebrating his life, such as THE SON OF MARY from
the HEAVEN SHALL NOT WAIT collection.

They were sitting on the ground,
four of them.
One couldn't walk,
one couldn't see,
one couldn't hear,
one couldn't be accepted in normal company
because he was different.

And a man came,
and sat among them
and talked to them,
and touched them,
especially the one who was different.
And he went away
leaving them all changed.

They were sitting on the ground,
four of them.
One was helpless,
one was disturbed,
one was concerned,
one was depressed,
and they looked at each other,
and they said to each other:
'Why does it happen?
Why does God let it happen?
It's a shame what people have to put up with.
What can *we* do?'

And the man came
and walked round them
and left them the same.
His eyes were on those who needed him,
not on those who complained about him.

Then someone came up and said,
'Are you the one who is to come?'

And he said:
'What do you see?
 What do you think?'

Today we remember, Lord

Prayer 9

Today we remember, Lord,
those who have yet to throw in their lot with you:

some enjoy talking about you,
  but would not risk talking to you;
some should be close by your side,
  but the wrong word at the right time
  from one of your followers
  has kept them at arm's length;
some are aflame with great ideas,
  but have yet to find the bridge
  from conviction to commitment.

For them we pray,
and for all who dither on the doorstep of discipleship,
that they may not fear to turn and face you
or take your hand
which is calloused with care.
AMEN.

Unthank
Script 11

To Jesus' hearers, it must have come as a shock to discover that the model of prayer which he encouraged was the unsophisticated few words of a social reject rather than the well-rehearsed and ostentatious offerings of a religious stalwart. But, as elsewhere in Jesus' ministry, he chose the forgotten or disregarded people to put in their place those who always had the centre stage.

In this script, which bears a passing resemblance to Dylan Thomas's UNDER MILK WOOD, we are enabled to eavesdrop on the evening devotions of different people in adjacent neighbourhoods.

For best effect, the script should be read in a darkened room with the various characters each holding a candle to illuminate their script and their person. After they have said their piece, they can blow out the candle. No movement is required, but it is good to have the various people located on the periphery of the hall or all round the front of an upstairs balcony, rather than sitting next to each other.

One variation might be to have Jackie Todd lie centrally in a bed; the person playing Jackie would have to memorise his/her script, thus enabling all to see him going to bed, putting off the light and saying his prayers.

It might also be possible to have an alarm go off to waken Jackie at the end, after which he could put on the light and maybe even get out of bed to say his morning prayer kneeling.

Characters can be omitted ad lib. To keep the performance time to within 15 minutes, Jason Vole and Mr & Mrs Meiklejohn can be omitted. However the location of the performance and social mix of the audience might suggest that other characters be omitted especially if, as might be the case with Jenny Morrison, a character too closely resembles one of the potential audience.

Because the script ends poignantly, applause is not necessarily the best thing to follow the 'Amen'. A song or music might better ensue.

Ref: Lk. 19:9–14

Narrator

Jackie Todd, *a dustman*

Molly McGhee, *a single lady*

Jason Vole, *a would-be clergyman, who intones*
his words

Herbert Spinks, *an accountant*

Jenny Morrison, *a former glamour-puss, preferably*
with an Irish accent

Gregory Thomson, *a schoolboy*

Mr & Mrs Meiklejohn, *a married couple who don't*
share everything about themselves

Olive Peabody, *an erudite upper-class lady*

Narrator: It is half past eleven of an autumn evening.

The big yellow moon,
like a bold, bald grandfather
unfurls its whiskers and smiles on the world,
and smiles particularly
on the dim and drowsy hamlet of Unthank.

One by one,
and one by one,
the house lights dim and douse
as young and old
and the very old
and the always-twenty-ones
pull on their Paisley patterns
or Marks and Spencer's winceyette,
and snuggle into teddy,
hubbie, wife or downie for the night.

And one by one,
and one by one,
when the mood takes them,
prayers are said by each
to the God they do or don't believe in.

Let us listen,
stealthily listen with the moon
for the murmurings of these sleepy spirits;
listen, say, in Glencraigs Gardens number 34,
where Jackie Todd, the dustman,
mumbles beneath a snore.

Jackie: *(Snore)*

Oh *(Snore)*
God, *(Snore)*
grant my heart's desire. *(Snore)*

Let me find a fortune *(Snore)*
so I can retire. *(Snore)*

Let me find an old antique
in a dirty rag, *(Snore)*
or better still a pot of gold
in a black bin bag. *(Snore)*

Narrator: Snore … snore …
while just next door,
all snuggled up
and curlers in at number 36,
Molly McGhee, a single lady,
makes a heartfelt plea for something shady.

Molly: God,
I want a man …
a rich one, if you can:
a man with a hairy chest
who refuses to wear a vest;
a man with mischief in his eyes …
oh, that would be a rare prize!
I'd even take Jackie Todd –
if he wasn't a dustman, God.

Narrator: Turn the corner with the smirking moon
and slither down the tiled roof
and under the eaves of 47 Bringham Grove,
where Jason Vole,
a would-be vicar,
rehearses his lines while the bedclothes snicker.

Jason: Dear Lord,
this is the 22nd Week in Pentecost
and, to tell you the truth,
I'm liturgically lost.

For I don't know what colour of piejams to wear –
is it green …
as in Trinity?

Or, since I'm aware
it's the feast of St Monica and St Ethelred,
maybe it's scarlet I should dress in for bed.

Dear Lord,
if I'm not in the proper church colour,
forgive me,
but I haven't got anything duller.

Narrator: Early to bed,
with the financial pages,
fifty-five-year-old Herbert Spinks,
who's read them for ages,
extinguishes, at long last,
his light
and drops to the floor at the side of his bed
to use the fond words which for all his life he's said.

Herbert: This night as I lie down to sleep
I pray the Lord my soul to keep …
and keep my stocks and shares as well.
With the latest threat of strikes, no one can tell
just where one's fortune can rest assured.
Still at least, thank God, I am fully insured
against wind and water, sickness and fraud,
unlike Mollie McGhee and Jackie Todd.

If I should die before I wake,
let no one know how much money I make,
in case they think I've bent some rules
or won a fortune on the pools.

But, if I survive for another day,
let the bank rate rise and the Chancellor stay.

Narrator: Thirty yards east, on the moonward side,
is the house of Jenny Morrison,
who, in ages past,
has been a teenage beauty queen.

But now,
through negligence rather than need,
Jenny's nubile figure
has somewhat gone to seed.

140

She has slipped to sleep
on her fireside armchair
and, while her lower dentures rest
on the tip of her chin,
her spirit sighs from the depth within.

Jenny: Hail Mary, full of grace,
I wish you would give me a brand new face;
remove the wrinkles from under my eyes
and 14 pounds from each of my thighs;
deflate the spare tyre round my waist
and give me new teeth so's I can taste
cream doughnuts and eclairs as they were meant,
instead of tainted with Steradent.

I'd like to appear like an hour glass
so that all would stare when I went to Mass.
And I'd like a new diet, which I could start on,
to give me a cleavage like Dolly Parton;
and I'd like two slices off my treble chin
so my neck wouldn't wobble whenever I grin;
and I'd like a jacuzzi in the corner of my room
and … blessed, oh Mary, is the fruit of your womb.

Narrator: Through Jenny's backyard and along Glassock Crescent,
fourth door on the right at the front upstairs,
seventeen-and-a-half-year-old Gregory Thomson
is trying not to say his prayers.

Gregory: God … I don't believe in you,
because Mr Jackson, the RE teacher,
does believe in you
and he looks miserable.

Now Mr McMurray, the art teacher,
he's an atheist,
and he's had three wives
and he goes to the bookie's at playtime
and he drives a Porsche;
and he's got long hair
even though most men at his age are bald.
And he looks much happier than Mr Jackson.
So I don't believe in you, God.
I think I'll get more out of life
being a heathen.

But …
if you are there …
could you do something about my spots
before Friday night?

Because I'm going to be an atheist,
I won't say Amen …
damn, I've just said it!

Oh … and PS, God,
I know I'm not doing very well at school,
but I still want to pass my exams.
I don't want to end up like Jackie Todd!

Narrator: The moon shines now on Newlands Place,
and on number 13, where, lucky for some,
Mr and Mrs Meiklejohn are having their quiet time …
each kneeling at a corner of the bed.

Mr M: I must say, God,
I only do this for the wife …

Mrs M: Thank you, Lord,
for such a truly pious husband …

Mr M: I wish I had never told her
about the Billy Graham rally.
That was in 1975 …

Mrs M: … who for the past 27 years
has been a model Christian …

Mr M: Well, I suppose I did feel something then.
But God, that was before the children
and the mortgage
and before they made me the personnel manager
and before I realised
that I didn't know how to pray.

Mrs M: Save me, Lord,
from being envious of my husband's faith.
I know he takes everything to you.

Mr M: I mean,
it's not that I don't believe,

it's just that I'm afraid to admit
that I'm not the perfect Christian
that Elizabeth over there thinks I am …

Mrs M: Lord, I know
that if Matthew had any idea
that I'm not the goody-goody he imagines me to be,
he'd probably leave me.

I do love him,
but sometimes I get fed up
being a kind of nice fairy
on the Christmas tree.

If only Matthew knew
that inside is a raging lion,
that I'm a tiger rather than a lamb …

Mr M: How long have we been down now …?
Three minutes …?
Let's give it another thirty seconds
and then I'll grunt 'Amen'.

OK, God …
I'll start counting …
1 … 2 … 3 … 4 …

Narrator: Five blocks away, among the 'private' houses,
hidden by rhododendrons, is no. 36 Castle Terrace.
There, in four-poster mahogany, dripping with hallelujahs,
Mrs Olive Peabody praises the Lord.

Olive: Almighty, invisible, inaccessible,
invincible, clothed in everlastingness,
enrobed in splendour, girded with glory,
inscrutable, incandescent, poly-magnificent,
gargantuan, gregorian, gyro-celestial,
neo-gothic, effervescent, multi-glutinous,
indestructible, biodegradable, ozone-friendly …

Oh Lord … what was I going to say?

(Pause)

I hope the bin man comes tomorrow.

Narrator: As the digitals revolve
and the hands chase each other
round Westclox, H. Samuel
and Thomas the Tank Engine faces,
the yellow-whiskered man or woman in the moon
gradually drops to dine on the first dew of the morning.

Then, at 4.30,
a rickety alarm springs to life
in Glencraigs Gardens,
and Jackie Todd opens his dusty eyes
and closes them again
to greet his Maker before the day begins.

Jackie: Lord, I dreamt last night
that I'd found my pot of gold,
but as soon as I touched it
my heart and hands went cold.

So I don't want to find any precious antique:
there are other things in life I know I should seek.

As today I lift the rubbish
from out a thousand bins,
will you lift from my life
all the grime, all the sins;
and make sure that this house
keeps an ever open door;
and make sure that my feet
walk the road they were meant for.
Amen.

Women on the way
Meditation 10

Since at Easter we celebrate how women were the first witnesses of the resurrection, it is appropriate to remember them in our preparation for the festival.

This script retells the stories of four women who showed the kind of faith in Jesus which he did not always find in men.

Each biblical incident is followed by a reflection either by the women concerned or by another interested party.

It is recommended that this script be used as the basis of either discussion or meditation. To enable that, it is suggested that the script be read with people sitting, if possible, in the round. With the Reader speaking from the periphery, a table in the centre should have four small unlit candles at different corners. After the biblical narrative, a symbol appropriate to the woman depicted can be placed next to the candle. After the reflection, the candle is lit.

It is best that one person places the symbols on the table and that the other person, or the reader of Jesus' part, lights each candle.

A verse of a hymn or song or a chant such as Taizé's UBI CARITAS or KINDLE A FLAME from the HEAVEN SHALL NOT WAIT collection may be sung as the candles are lit.

One appropriate way of following the script is to move into a time of prayer where the leader simply asks people to pray for women, using the categories alluded to in the script.

Ref: Lk.10:38–42 (Martha); Jn.4:1–41 (the woman at the well); Mk.5:25–34, Lk.8:43–48 (the haemorrhaging woman); Jn.12:1–8 (Mary)

Personnel: **Narrator**
Jesus
Martha
Noreen, the woman at the well
Cassie, the haemorrhaging woman
Disciple
Judas

Narrator: Jesus and his disciples came to a village
where a woman named Martha
welcomed him to her house.
She had a sister named Mary,
who sat down at the feet of the Lord
and listened to his teaching.

Martha was upset
over all the work she had to do,
so she came to Jesus and said,

Martha: Lord, don't you care
that my sister has left me
to do all the work by myself?
Tell her to come and help me!

Narrator: Jesus answered her,

Jesus: Martha, Martha,
you are worried and troubled
over so many things,
but just one thing is needed.

Mary has chosen the right thing
and it will not be taken away from her.

(A duster is placed centrally)

Martha: Well, that's my gas in a peep (*me put in my place*).
And for what?
For doing my best!

You know what it's like
when somebody comes …
you vacuum the carpet,
you brush the stairs,
you get out the wedding china.

And then there's baking to be done
and I never get the scones to rise
if I'm in a hurry.

And my mother always told us
when we were lassies (*girls*)
that when a visitor came,
to put on a clean apron.

146

So I'm in the middle of all this,
and I'm up to high doh,
and our Mary's sitting
like a lodging house cat
and …

Jesus: Martha, did you hear what I said?

The dust and the pancakes
and the scatter cushions
will come and go.

And there will be more housework
and baking
and tidying up
to take their place.

In the middle of your panic,
have you no time for what really lasts?

(A candle is lit as the chant is sung)

Narrator: Jesus came,
by himself,
to Jacob's Well in the town of Sychar.
He was tired and sat down about noon.

A Samaritan woman came to draw some water
and Jesus said to her,

Jesus: Can I have a drink of water?

Narrator: The woman answered,

Noreen: You are a Jew,
I'm a Samaritan.
How can you ask me for a drink?

Jesus: If only you knew what God gives
and who was asking you for a drink,
you would ask him
and he would give you life-giving water,
and you would never be thirsty again.

Noreen: Sir, can I have some of that water?

Jesus: Go and call your husband and come back.

147

Noreen: I haven't got a husband.

Jesus: You're right.
You've had five,
and the man you have now isn't your husband.

Noreen: I see that you're a prophet.
And I know that when the Messiah comes,
he'll tell us everything.

Jesus: I am he,
I who am talking with you now.

(A pitcher is placed centrally)

Noreen: Well what could I say?

Harry's lying in his bed,
waiting for me to come back and make the dinner,
and I'm standing blethering to another man …
another man!
… as if I'd not had enough trouble with men.

And he's a Jew.
And we don't talk to them.

But this Jew …
(I wonder what Harry would say
if he heard I was talking to a Jew …)

Anyway, this Jew …
I don't think I've ever talked to a man
who understood me.
I mean,
men don't understand women,
but this man understood me.

It was as if
everything I've never been able to tell Harry,
I could tell him …
even the things
I don't like admitting to myself.

It was just like saying
the best prayer of my life,
and having it answered there and then.

(A candle is lit as the chant is sung)

Narrator: As Jesus was walking along,
people were crowding him on every side.

Among them was a woman
who had suffered terribly
from severe bleeding for twelve years.

She had spent all her money on cures,
but instead of getting better, she got worse.

She heard about Jesus,
so she tried to get near him,
saying to herself,

Cassie: If I just touch his clothes,
I'll get better.

Narrator: She touched his clothes
and her bleeding stopped at once.
And she had the feeling,
inside herself,
that she was healed of her trouble.

At once,
Jesus knew that power had gone out of him,
so he turned round in the crowd and asked,

Jesus: Who touched my clothes?

Narrator: His disciples answered,

Disciple: You see how many people are crowding you!
Why do you ask who touched you?

Narrator: But Jesus kept turning round
to see who had done it.

The woman realised what had happened to her,
so she came,
trembling with fear,
knelt at his feet,
and told him the whole truth.

Jesus said to her,

Jesus: My daughter,
your faith has made you well.

Go in peace,
and be healed of your trouble.

(A bandage is placed centrally)

Cassie: You don't know what it's like.
You don't know what it feels like
and you don't know what it's been like.

Most women are bothered with bleeding
once a month.
I bled every day,
every day for twelve years.

Some days I would just lie in my bed
and try not to stand up.
But it never worked.

Nor did the doctors.
I've been from doctor to specialist,
haematologist to gynaecologist;
and always the same questions:
How long have you been like this?
When did it start?
What brings it on?
Your family history?
Your diet?

I became a medical curio,
someone on whom the doctors
tested their theories
and tried the latest drug.

And I realised that to them
my disease was more important than me.

But what cured me was finding the man
who believed that I was more important
than the disease.
And all I did
was reach out to touch him.

(A candle is lit as the chant is sung)

150

Narrator: Six days before the Passover,
Jesus went to Bethany,
to the house of Lazarus.

They prepared a dinner for him
which Martha helped to serve,
and Lazarus sat close to Jesus at the table.

Then Mary took half a litre
of very expensive perfume
made of pure nard.

She poured it on Jesus' feet
and wiped them with her hair.

The sweet smell of the perfume
filled the whole house.

At this, Judas said,

Judas: Why wasn't the perfume sold for three hundred silver coins
and the money given to the poor?

Narrator: He said this,
not because he cared for the poor,
but because he was a thief.
He carried the money bag
and helped himself from it.

Jesus said to him,

Jesus: Leave her alone!
Let her keep what she has
for the day of my burial.

You will always have the poor with you
but you won't always have me.

(Perfume is placed centrally)

Judas: I don't care what he says,
I think it's a waste.

But, of course,
it's a habit of his.

Wherever there's something going for nothing,
he takes it.

I've seen us just walking into a town
and some heathen asks him
to come in to his house for a meal.

So in he goes and plunks himself down,
and then comes away with some rubbish
about how you have to receive
what the poor have to offer.

This is a pretty good week for getting treated.

On Sunday he got a civic reception,
banners, big cheers, the works.

Yesterday the children sang for him
and he was as pleased as punch.

Tonight he's getting a four-course meal
and perfume on his feet.

And I have got it on good authority
that somebody has laid on another banquet
for Thursday.

But draw all this to his attention
and he'll excuse the extravagance
without a thought …
'The gifts of the poor … the gifts of the poor …'

It makes me sick.

If that stupid woman gave me her perfume,
I'd sell it for a fortune.

Then I could feed the poor
and buy her a bracelet with the money,
and she would have that
long after he's dead.

(A candle is lit as the chant is sung)

152

You broke down the barriers
Prayer 10

Ref: 1 Cor.12:12–13, Gal.3:28, Col.3:11

Leader: You broke down the barriers
when you crept in beside us.
For in Jesus,
the smiling Jesus,
the story-telling Jesus,
the controversial Jesus,
the annoying Jesus,
the loving and forgiving Jesus,
your hands touched all
and touched us,
showing how in Christ,
there is neither Jew nor Gentile,
neither male nor female;

ALL: ALL ARE ONE IN JESUS CHRIST
AND FOR THIS WE PRAISE YOU.

Leader: You opened our eyes
to see how the hands of the rich were empty
and the hearts of the poor were full.
You dared to take the widow's mite,
the young boy's loaves,
the child at the breast,
and in these simple things,
point out the path to your kingdom.

You said 'Follow me,
for on your own you will never discover
that in Christ there is neither Jew nor Gentile,
neither male nor female';

ALL: ALL ARE ONE IN JESUS CHRIST
AND FOR THIS WE PRAISE YOU.

Leader: You gave us hands to hold –
              black hands and brown hands,
              African hands and Asian hands,
              the clasping hands of lovers,
              the reluctant hands of those
              who don't believe they are worth holding.

              And when we wanted to shake our fist,
              you still wanted to shake our hand,
              because in Christ there is neither Jew nor Gentile,
              neither male nor female;
ALL: ALL ARE ONE IN JESUS CHRIST
              AND FOR THIS WE PRAISE YOU.

Leader: Here in the company of the neighbour whom we know,
              and the stranger in our midst,
              and the self from whom we turn,
              we ask to love as Jesus loved.
              Make this the place and time, good Lord,
              when heaven and earth merge into one,
              and we in word and flesh can grasp
              that in Christ there is neither Jew nor Gentile,
              neither male nor female;
ALL: ALL ARE ONE IN JESUS CHRIST
              AND FOR THIS WE PRAISE YOU.

You will not always have me
Meditation 11

Here one of the disciples reflects on the events leading up to Jesus' being anointed by Mary. It may be preceded by DISCIPLES OF CHRIST (page 76) and followed by a depiction of the story in movement, dance or a symbolic action, such as ANOINTING in the STAGES ON THE WAY collection.

Ref: Matt.26:6–13, Mk.14:3–9, Jn.12:1–8

Personnel: **Reader**, *a disciple*
Jesus

Reader: He had never said that kind of thing before …

Jesus: You will not always have me.

Reader: He had warned us about Jerusalem,
about going up to the city,
about how he would be hounded
and rounded on …
and other things which we did not want to hear.

But this was Bethany.

Jesus: You will not always have me.

Reader: Who did he say it to?
That was the problem.
We could not all see,
the room was crowded,
and other people were talking.

It was not as if time stood still
and everyone froze to watch the action.

No, no.
James and John were arguing – as ever,
a woman with a demented daughter
was screaming for attention,
Martha was shouting for help in the kitchen
and somebody who was allergic to olives
was vomiting in a corner.

Jesus: You will not always have me.

Reader: Some of us thought he said it to Mary.

There had been talk …
well, there was always talk …

She doted on him,
hung on his every word.

So maybe it was his way of telling her to back off,
to put clear limits on their relationship,
to say,
'That's enough Mary.
There are others you should attend to.
I've got more to do than be feted by you …'

Jesus: You will not always have me.

Reader: But more of us thought he was talking to Judas.

For Judas was a rat.
He was the kind of guy
who was so smug that it made you suspicious.

You know the kind of person who is always saying
the church isn't doing enough for the poor
but who would never put a penny in a begging bowl?
… that was Judas.

He was our treasurer.
He always complained that we didn't have enough money.
He suggested one day that if Jesus cured somebody,
we should ask for a donation.

And he would have pilfered every penny
if Matthew hadn't kept an eye on him.

156

So we thought it was him that Jesus was talking to,
telling him that there were plenty of opportunities
to exercise his concern for the poor …
if only he would take them.

Or was he,
in his own way,
telling Judas that he knew what he was up to,
and that both their days were numbered?

Jesus: You will not always have me.

Reader: Or was he speaking to us, to all of us.

Was he giving us a last chance
to say or to show whether we loved him?

And maybe that's what made us jealous of Mary.

Because she showed she cared.
And the rest of us presumed we didn't need to tell him.

I remember thinking:
if my mother was dying,
I'd give her all the time I could,
I would take her a red rose
and tell her that I loved her.
I would read her the psalms she wanted to hear
and sing the songs she had taught me as a child.

And here –
with Jesus making clear he was soon to leave us –
what did we give him?
What did we tell him?
Why did we hold back?

Jesus: You will not always have me.

(Link to symbolic action)

The way of Jesus

A question of technique
Script 12

In this conversation, Peter grills Jesus about the technique he uses to heal people.

Ref: Lk.4:40

Personnel: **Peter**
Jesus

Peter: Eh … Jesus …?

Jesus: Yes, Peter?

Peter: Can I ask you a question about your technique?

Jesus: What technique, Peter?

Peter: I was afraid you would say that.

Jesus: What's this about?

Peter: It's just that the disciples and I
were trying to work out
what your technique was for healing people.

Jesus: What did you come up with?

Peter: Well, at first we thought it was to do with your hands.

Because when you healed Jairus' daughter
and my old mother-in-law,
you took them by the hand.

But then we remembered the woman
who had been bleeding for twelve years.
You never touched her.

So we decided it wasn't your hands.

Jesus: Well done.
Was there another theory?

Peter: Yes.
Martha thought it was your voice.
Because when you raised Lazarus,
you shouted at him and he came back to life.

But then Andrew reminded us
of how you never saw the centurion's servant,
but you managed to bring him back to life
without shouting.

Jesus: So, you decided that it couldn't be my voice.

Peter: That's right.

Oh, Jesus, we even thought
it might be something to do with your saliva.

Jesus: My saliva?

Peter: Well, you did spit on the deaf man's tongue
and that started him yapping
as if it was going out of fashion.

And you spat on mud at the pool of Siloam
and you rubbed the mixture on the blind boy's eyes.

Jesus: But I've healed other deaf people,
and I cured Bartimaeus without spitting.

Peter: Oh, Thomas reminded us of that.

So, the saliva theory is out the window.

Jesus: So, what conclusion did you come to
about my technique?

Peter: Jesus, we don't think you have one!

Jesus: Right fourth time!
I don't have a technique.

Peter: Then how do you heal?

Jesus: Peter,
when Andrew and you were wee (*little*) boys,
did your mother always treat you the same?

Peter: Oh yes.
She had no favourites.

Jesus: I'm not asking you if she had favourites.
I'm asking you if she treated you the same.

Peter: Well … yes and no.

Jesus: Tell me about the 'no'.

Peter: Let me think …
(Hesitates)
oh yes, here's an example.

If my mother wanted us to get up in the morning,
she would tell Andrew it was half past seven
and me it was half past eight.

Jesus: Why was that?

Peter: Because she knew
that Andrew loved getting up and I hated it.

The only way she could ever get me out of my bed
was to convince me that I was late.

Jesus: Your mother, Peter,
is like God.

Peter: Don't be daft, Jesus,
my mother wears dentures!

Jesus: Peter, your mother is like God.

In order to get you changed
from your pyjamas to your shirt and trousers,
she had to treat you as an individual.

When God, through me,
changes people from being sick to being healthy,
it doesn't happen because of a slick technique.

When you love people,
you treat them and heal them
as individuals.

A sower went out to sow
Meditation 12

Here the parable of the sower is explored. A, B and C sit on the circumference of the assembly, D in the midst.

Ref: Matt.13:1–9, 18–23; Mk.4:1–9, 13–20; Lk.8:4–8, 11–15

Personnel: **Narrator**
             A, a path
             B, a rock garden
             C, the waste land
             D, the fertile soil

Narrator: This is a story of Jesus:
                a sower went out to sow …

A: And the first seed fell on me.
                And I am a path,
                I am easily walked over;
                people do that all the time.

                I have no identity of my own.
                And should anything fall on me,
                others will pick it up,
                like birds scrambling for crumbs,
                and I am left bare and fruitless.

                I am the one people walk over.

Narrator: This is a story of Jesus:
                a sower went out to sow …

B: And the second seed fell on me.
                And I am a rock garden,
                Attractive but shallow.

                People admire me all the time.
                They say how good I look
                and I like looking good.

165

They say what novel ideas I have
and I like having novel ideas.
The trouble is they are always novel,
always new.
Here today, withered tomorrow,
no root … no depth …
but admirable in a shallow way.

Narrator: This is a story of Jesus:
a sower went out to sow …

C: And the third seed fell on me.
And I am the waste land
on which weeds thrive.

I am filled with 'isms':
commercialism, materialism,
consumerism, industrialism,
capitalism, communism.

I am full of theory
and barren of life,
choking to death everything real.

I am the waste land,
full of 'isms',
none of them working.

Narrator: This is a story of Jesus:
a sower went out to sow …

D: And we are the fertile soil
to whom he gives much,
from whom he expects much.

(Silence)

Narrator: And on the good soil
the seed fell and produced plants.
And the plants ripened and produced grain …
thirtyfold
and sixtyfold
and a hundredfold.

And Jesus said,
'If you have ears to hear,
then hear.'

And lest we disown the past
or forget the future
and covet the present,
Jesus also said,
'What someone else sowed you are reaping.
And what you sow someone else will reap.'

And that is the way
the kingdom comes:
the seed from God
and the cooperation from God's people.

As those who have been touched

Prayer 11

During this prayer a chant such as the Ukrainian Orthodox KYRIE (from the MANY & GREAT collection) may be sung.

Personnel: **A**
            B

A: As those who have been touched by your Son,
as those who have been awakened by your Spirit
as those who have come together out of conviction,
and yet as those who –
despite our spiritual pedigree –
are empty vessels waiting to be filled,
we ask for your grace and your mercy O God.

ALL: *(Sung response – KYRIE)*

A: Where our familiarity with the Gospel
has desensitised us to its demanding truth;
where our relationship with Christ
has become more nostalgic than dynamic;
where we have lost our first love
and become lukewarm,
we ask for your grace and your mercy, O God.

ALL: *(Sung response – KYRIE)*

A: Where we have regarded mission as what we do,
rather than what Christ does;
where we have regarded mission
as the prerogative of the strong
rather than the gift of the weak;
where our hands have been quick to give,
but our hearts reluctant to receive,
we ask for your grace and your mercy, O God.

ALL: *(Sung response – KYRIE)*

A: On us,
in us,
for us,
through us,
around us,
before us,
and – if need be – despite us,
we ask for your grace and your mercy, O God.

ALL: *(Sung response – KYRIE)*

B: Listen,
for these are the words of Jesus Christ
and they can be trusted:

'I did not come to call the righteous,
but sinners.

Whoever does God's will
is my mother and sister and brother.

Never mind what the others do …
you … follow me.'

A: Thanks be to God
who meets and mends us in Jesus.
AMEN.

Be on your guard
Meditation 13

This reading may precede or follow a reading of the Gospel. According to circumstance, the allusions to war and tyranny may be changed. At the beginning and/or the end, it may be appropriate for the worship leader to offer comment or make some observations about the issues raised.

Ref: Matt.24:4–8

Personnel: **Reader**
A
B
C

(Optional comment by worship leader)

Reader: Jesus said,
'Be on your guard
and do not let anyone deceive you.
Many men, claiming to speak for me,
will come and say,
"I am the Messiah,"
and they will deceive many people.'

A: That's what Hitler did,
and deceived the German nation
and murdered six million Jews.

B: That's what Mussolini did,
and deceived the Italian nation
and helped the fascist holocaust.

C: That's what Franco did,
and deceived the Spanish nation,
slaughtering those who disagreed with him.

A: It's what Stalin did,
abolishing religion
and replacing it with the State.

B: It's what Mao did,
          turning himself into a god
          and annihilating his opponents.

C: It's what Kim did in North Korea,
          it's what Hussein did in Iraq,
          it's what Banda did in Malawi,
          it's what Reagan did in Nicaragua,
          all pretending that they were the Messiah,
          all saying that God was on their side,
          all murdering those who thought differently.

Reader: Jesus said,
             'You will hear of wars close at hand,'

A: The war against racism,

B: the war against unemployment,

C: the war against tax evasion,

A: the war against organised crime,

B: the war against drug-pushing,

C: the war against child abuse.

Reader: 'And you will hear rumours of wars far away.'

A: In Bosnia,

B: in Rwanda,

C: in East Timor,

A: in Kuwait,

B: in Angola,

C: in Afghanistan.

Reader: 'But do not be troubled.
             Such things must happen,
             but it does not mean the end has come.
             Countries will attack each other,
             kingdoms will fight each other.'

A: The Chinese against Tibet,

B: Muslim fundamentalists against the Christians in Nigeria,

C: the Israelis against the Palestinians.

Reader: 'There will be famine ...'

A: In Ethiopia,

B: in the Sudan,

C: on the Thames embankment.

Reader: '... and earthquakes,'

A: in California,

B: in India,

C: in the Philippines.

Reader: 'But these things
are like the first pains of childbirth.'

(Optional comment by worship leader)

Christ's food in our souls

Closing responses 2

Leader: Christ's food in our souls,
ALL: OUR FOOD SHARED LIKE HIS.

Leader: Christ's life in our hands,
ALL: OUR LIVES SHAPED BY HIS.

Leader: Christ's love in our hearts,
ALL: OUR LOVE WARMED THROUGH HIS.

Leader: Christ's peace on our path,
ALL: OUR PATH FOLLOWING HIS.
AMEN.

Diva and Zara
Script 13

One of Jesus' most uncompromising parables is that of Dives and Lazarus, the story of the rich man who never saw the beggar at his gate. 'Diva and Zara' simply retells the original parable in a contemporary setting, using female rather than male characters.

We do not feel that this in any way detracts from the original purpose. Indeed, there are a number of occasions when Jesus told parables with a common point using complementary male and female images. The Lost Coin and The Lost Sheep are good examples of this.

When using this script, it is good to have a Narrator positioned centrally, like a story-teller, with everyone in view. Where the other characters are located depends entirely on the physical possibilities of the building. Ideally it would be good to have Diva and Marcella on a side balcony with Zara and Betty appearing below it. They could later reappear, with Sarah, on an opposite balcony. What is essential is that in the first half there should be close proximity between Diva and Zara. In the second half there should be a considerable distance.

Music may be used midway to alter the mood and enable Zara and Diva to change position.

Ref: Lk.16:19–31

Personnel: **Narrator**
          Diva, *a lady of wealth and privilege*
          Marcella, *her maid*
          Zara, *a homeless woman recently released 'into the community' from a sanatorium*
          Betty, *her companion*
          Sarah, *mother of Isaac and wife of Abraham*

Narrator: There was once a rich woman
who dressed in expensive clothes and …

Diva: *(Interrupting)*
I wouldn't say I dressed in 'expensive' clothes,
but admittedly they don't come from a nearly new shop.

Narrator: who dressed in expensive clothes,
and lived in great luxury …

Diva: *(Interrupting)*
I wouldn't say I lived in 'great luxury',
just because Harrods is handy.
I mean, if there were a Sainsbury's,
perhaps one would shop there for pet food.

Narrator: … and lived in great luxury every day.

Diva: Marcella, remind me where I'm due this morning.

Marcella: There's an aromatherapy appointment at 10.00, ma'am,
then morning coffee with Lady Gainsborough
in Liberty's at 11.00.

You're going to discuss colours
for the decor of the summer house
with the interior designer at 11.45,
and then Sir Arnold is picking you up at 12.15
to take you to lunch at Claridges.

Diva: Is this the Press Association lunch, Marcella?

Marcella: No, ma'am. It's the Dulwich Hospice Appeal.

Diva: Then I'd better wear grey with the foxfurs.
One does want to be respectful
of the potentially dying.

Narrator: There was also a poor woman called Zara,
covered with scabs and sores.

Every day she was helped up
from the Thames embankment,
where she slept,
to the door of the rich woman's house.

(Zara appears, helped by Betty)

Zara: Thanks, Betty.

Betty: OK, Zara …
I'll be back for you in the afternoon.

Zara: You know, Betty …
I wasn't always like this.
I was never like this in hospital.

Betty: What hospital was that, Zara?

Zara: Oh, I don't know …
some hospital in Birmingham.

They say my mother was put into it
when she went mad after having me.
So I was brought up in a locked ward.

And when they saw that I was epileptic,
they kept me in …
even after my mother died.

Betty: Why was that?

Zara: There was nobody to look after me.
And who would want
to adopt an eight-year-old epileptic
from an asylum?

Betty: How long did you stay there?

Zara: Until a few years ago.

Nobody ever thought
what else could be done with me
and I had nowhere to go.

Betty: But you're an intelligent woman, Zara.

Zara: That's what one of the doctors used to say, Betty.
He would say …
'You're an intelligent woman, Zara.'

Betty: But they never let you out?

Zara: No …
and nobody ever told me I could get out.
Until they got the word they had to shut wards
and reduce beds,
and I was given a case and told to start packing.

Betty: Where did you go, Zara?

Zara: Some hostel for women.
It was supposed to be just temporary.
But when they saw me taking fits,
they threw me out.

They said they couldn't cope with medical problems
and that I was scaring the other people in the hostel.

Betty: So where did you go?

Zara: They told me
to go to the Homeless Person's Unit or something.

But, Betty,
I had never been in Birmingham on my own.

So I came to London on a bus.
I had seen it on the television.
I thought I would like it better
because I knew it.

Betty: And it didn't work out … eh?

Zara: No, Betty.
But at least I've got a friend here.

Betty: We're all friends
when you get to the bottom, Zara.

(Pause)

Now I'll away and see what's what.
I'll be back at four,
and then we'll go to the Sally Army
for some soup.

(Betty goes off)

Narrator: The poor woman would sometimes crawl
to the rich woman's dustbins
to see if there were scraps of food
she might salvage for herself and her friends.

And sometimes when she slept,
dogs would come and lick her arms and legs,
for they were covered with sores.

Diva: Marcella …
look out the window!

Is that Candy?
Call her in.
She's over at that old tramp again.

You never know what she might catch.
In fact arrange for the vet to see her …
just as a precaution.

Marcella: Yes, ma'am.

Diva: Marcella …
was Sir Arnold not going to telephone the authorities
about these street people?

That one seems to sit at our gate Monday to Friday
as if it were her full-time job.

Something should be done about her …

Needless to say,
she'll not be paying any taxes.
They're just parasites these people!
That's what the welfare state has bred.

*(Zara removes herself and gets repositioned as music plays.
She may also slightly alter her appearance)*

Narrator: In time, the poor woman died
and was carried by the angels
to sit beside Sarah in the feast of heaven.

Sarah: Hello … are you Zara?

Zara: Yes …

Sarah: I'm Sarah.
Maybe you'll have heard of my husband, Abraham.

Zara: No …
I never knew anyone called Abraham.
Wait a minute …
where am I?

Sarah: Heaven.

Zara: Heaven?
Me in heaven?
But I'm a tramp …
and I'm an epileptic …
and I'm in a mess …
and I never went to church …

Sarah: Zara …
look in the mirror.

(Sarah may hold a mirror up to Zara)

You're not how you were.
You are how you were always meant to be …
a child of God.

And this is God's house,
and you are going to sit next to me
at God's table.

Narrator: The rich woman also died and was buried,
and in the place of the dead,
where she was in great pain,
she looked up and saw Sarah far away
with Zara at her side.

Diva: Sarah …
Saint Sarah …
Mother Sarah …
look …
look with mercy …

This is Diva …
Diva …
remember me … ?

I was a respectable woman …
married to Sir Arnold …
you know him.

I never did a soul any harm.

I was a member of St Mary Magdalen's;
I sang in the choir when I was a little girl;
I used to collect for the Earl Haig Fund;
I played whist for the Dulwich Hospice.

I don't deserve to be here.
Gabriel must have got it wrong.

Dear Sarah …
take pity on me …
send that lovely angel beside you
to dip her finger in some water
and come to cool my tongue.
I can't stand the heat …
I can't stand the fire.

Narrator: Sarah heard Diva's plea …
and she replied …

Sarah: Remember, my daughter,
that in your lifetime
you were given all the good things
while Zara had all the bad.

Now she is enjoying herself here
while you are in pain.

Once only a few feet separated you from her.
You could have walked over,
fed her,
clothed her,
bandaged her,
put her on her feet again.

But you never did.

Now there is a deep pit lying between her and you.
No one from here who wants to
can cross over to you;

and no one who wants to
can cross over from your side to us.

Narrator: Then the rich woman replied …

Diva: Saint Sarah …
Mother Sarah …
I beg you …
send that angel to where I came from.

I have five sisters and lots of friends.

Let her warn them
about what to do and what not to do …

Let her tell them about feeding the hungry
and clothing the naked,
and visiting the prisoners
and caring for the poor.

Let her warn them
about the dangers of affluence,
so that my sisters and friends
might not follow me to this place of pain.

Sarah: Listen, my daughter,
your sisters have had Hannah,
Miriam, Ruth, Naomi,
Rahab, Martha, Mary,
Clare, Teresa
and a host of others to warn them,
teach them,
encourage them.

Let your sisters listen
to what they have to say.

Diva: Not enough!
It is not enough, Mother Sarah.

What they need
is someone from the other side of time …
someone to come back from the grave,
to convince them that heaven and hell are real …
someone to rise from the dead.

Then they would believe
and change their ways.

Sarah: Listen …
if they pay no attention to the sisters in God
who speak the truth among them,
they would not be convinced
even if someone were to rise from the grave.

Narrator: And then silence reigned
over the rich woman, Diva,
who thirsted and hungered
in the place of the dead.

But at God's table,
Zara sat and ate and sang,
and the sight and sound of her
warmed the heart of God.

Four changed lives

Meditations 14

This is a straightforward sequence of personal testimonies to the transforming power of Jesus. It may be followed by a conversation initiated by a question such as 'Which of these four people featured in the Gospels would you like to meet, and what would you ask them?'

Ref: Lk.10:38–42 (Martha); Mk.2:1–12, Lk.5:17–26 (the paralysed man); Matt.19:16–30, Mk.10:17–31, Lk.18:18–30 (the rich young man); Jn.4:1–41 (the woman by the well)

Personnel: **Martha**, *sister of Mary and Lazarus*
                  Jesus
                  Brebo, *a paralysed man*
                  Jethro, *a rich young man*
                  Lois, *the woman by the well*

Martha: I have always known my place.

I was the oldest in the family.
I didn't have my brother's brains
or my sister's good looks.
But in any case, they were young
when my mother died
and I had to take her place.

I did all the cooking and baking and laundry
the way my mother had done
and I kept the books,
because my father was useless with money.

And people admired me.
They'd say,
'Your father doesn't know how lucky he is
to have a girl like you in the house.'

Or they'd say,
'You'll make a great wife
for some lucky man, Martha.'

But there was no lucky man,
and when my father died,
I just kept house for the other two.

I had no money of my own,
only what the other two gave me;
and my friends were mostly
of the older generation.

But I knew my place ...
I knew it from the day my mother died
and I took over in the kitchen,
and I welcomed everyone at the door
and brought them in
and made them comfortable
and started baking and ...

Jesus: Martha, Martha,
you're fussing and fretting
about so many things.
The place Mary has chosen is best
and it won't be taken away from her.

Martha: So I changed ...
I changed places ...
I moved from the outside to the inside.
And I didn't feel comfortable.
I'm only just getting used to it.

Brebo: When some people
have been lying in bed for eight hours,
they get restless.

They want to get up.
They feel guilty about enjoying their rest.

When most people have been ill
or had an operation,
they can't wait to get up.
It's a sign that they're on the mend.
They want to show what they can do ...

184

and there are some doctors
who would encourage that.
They reckon that lying still
does more harm to the system than good.

But when you've been lying in bed
for ten years,
when you've been paralysed
from the neck down,
when you've been fed and toiletted
by your mother and father,
as if you were a baby …

when you've been lying in bed
for ten years,
you'd think you'd be desperate to get up.

Don't believe it.
You're scared stiff.

Listen, I didn't ask to be cured.

I was not the one who
asked for a stretcher party
or organised the dismantling of the roof
or gave directions
for lowering me into a crowded room,
like a coffin being laid in a grave.

It was them that did it.

Jesus: Stand up.
lift up your bed …
and go home.

Brebo: So what do I say …
about me …
and about him?

And how do I learn to do all the things
that other folk have done for me?

And how can you cope with the outside world
if you've lived all your life
inside yourself?

When you change a cripple into a jogger,
it's more than his legs you change …
it's everything.

Jethro: I suppose after what you've heard –
this will be a bit of an anti-climax.

There has been no movement,
though there was at first.

You see, I ran.
Yes, I ran, out of breath and eager.

And when he stopped,
I smiled and he smiled
and it was just like meeting someone
you hadn't seen for ages
and we got right into the conversation.

No small talk.
I just asked him the question.

And why not? I'm confident,
I can present or defend an argument
when I need to.

I'm not intimidated by philosophers
or folk-heroes.

What was disarming
was the way he replied to me.

I mean, if he had frowned
or been dismissive or shouted,
I'd know how to respond.

But he looked at me
as if he were about to weep.

He looked at me,
bubbling full of enthusiasm,
as if he were about to cry.

Jesus: Go and sell what you have.
Give it to the poor
and come and follow me.

Jethro: There has been no movement since.
I am numb.

I don't understand.
I was all ready for an inner journey
and he asked me to go on an outward one.

It was six weeks ago …
and I just still feel numb.

Lois: I used to go to fortune-tellers,
not often …
maybe once a year.
I tried different ones,
usually with my eye on 'romantic prospects'.

They clearly read me like a book;
my face must have looked
like an advertisement in the personal columns:
unhappy in present relationship,
desperately seeking a partner
who will understand.

I believed I could do nothing
to change the future.
It all had to happen.
It was in the stars.

And so whenever a man drifted my way,
I saw him as if blown in
by the wind of fate,
and I welcomed him into my bed,
where he stayed
until either he set his sights
on something more attractive,
or I got fed up with being abused …
again …

But I thought it was all in the stars,
I couldn't change the future.

And then I met a man
who told me nothing about my future,
but everything about my past,
while he waited for …

Jesus: Could you give me a drink of water?

Lois: He didn't read my face,
he read my heart,
and it was as if he told me my story,
and felt my pain
at being rejected so often,
and recognised the good things in me
which I was scared to admit to.

I had introduced my 'men friends' to people before,
and behind my back they called me a slut.

But when I introduced this man
to the people in my street,
they called me an evangelist.

You see, when I talked to him
I felt for the first time in my life
that I was understood.

I knew that I had been immoral.
I knew I was guilty
of letting down my family,
I knew I had degraded myself …
I knew all that.

But I never knew
what it was like to be understood.

I never knew what it was like
to be known inside out.

Home town sermon
Script 14

This is a simple depiction of the disruption caused by Jesus' first sermon in his home synagogue. Any worship space is suitable and the only accessories are a scroll and loud organ or other noises to accompany his eviction. A, B, C and D should be seated in the midst of the assembly.

Ref: Matt.13:53–58, Mk.6:1–6, Lk.4:16–30

Personnel: **Narrator**
Attendant
Jesus
A
B
C
D

Narrator: Jesus stood up to read

(He stands)

and the scroll of the prophet Isaiah
was given to him.

(Scroll is given to Jesus by the Attendant)

He unrolled the scroll

(Unrolls scroll)

and found the place
where it is written:

Jesus: The Spirit of the Lord is upon me …
because he has anointed me
to bring good news to the poor.

He has sent me to proclaim release to the captives
and recovery of sight to the blind,
to let the oppressed go free,
to proclaim the year of the Lord's favour.

Narrator: Then he rolled up the scroll

(Rolls up scroll)

and gave it back to the attendant

(Gives it back)

and sat down.

(Sits)

The eyes of the synagogue were fixed on him.

(Jesus takes a long time to look round)

Jesus: Today …
today, this scripture is fulfilled in your hearing.

A: Well, isn't that amazing!

B: He reads very well, doesn't he?

C: That boy will go a long way!

D: Is he not Joseph's son?
Is that not his mother and family sitting over there?

Jesus: Doubtless, you will quote the proverb,
'Doctor, heal yourself!'
And you'll also want to say,
'Do in your hometown what you did in Capernaum.'

Let me tell you the truth:
no prophet … *no prophet* …
is accepted in his hometown.

The truth is that there were
a lot of widows in Israel when Elijah was about.
The skies were shut up for three and a half years
and there was a terrible famine.

190

But who was Elijah sent to?
Not to any of the Jewish widows.
He was sent to Zarapeth … in Sidon.

And then when Elisha was around,
there were plenty of lepers in Israel.

But which one of them was cleansed? …
none … *none* …
only Naaman … who came from Syria.

Narrator: When the congregation heard this,
all the synagogue was filled with rage.

*(Chaotic organ sounds as Jesus' removal is enacted. The
four speakers – A, B, C and D – rush towards him shouting
phrases such as 'Out! Out!' or 'Enough! This is a blasphemy!'
etc. as they evict Jesus from the room)*

They got up and drove him out of town.

They took him to the brow of the hill
on which the town was built
so that they could throw him over the cliff.

But Jesus passed through the midst of them
and went on his way.

Homes and houses
Prayer 12

This prayer may be used with THERE IS ONE AMONG US (page 130) or on its own.

Let us pray.

Come to our houses, Lord Jesus …

to the tables where we eat,
and the places where we argue,
and the rooms where we sleep
or lie awake,
wondering if our life is worthwhile.

Come to our houses
to broaden our hospitality
and deepen our conversation
and keep our souls company.

And come to our houses of prayer,
to save our churches
from being so absorbed with what needs to be done,
that our plans have no place
for any hint of salvation
or of all things being made new.

And come to this place
as week by week we meet,
and show us the cross we must carry
so that we may be shaped by your love.
AMEN.

In gratitude, in deep gratitude
Closing responses 3

Leader: In gratitude, in deep gratitude
for this moment,
this place,
these people,
we give ourselves to you.

ALL: TAKE US OUT
TO LIVE AS CHANGED PEOPLE,
BECAUSE WE HAVE BEEN TOUCHED BY THE LIVING LORD
AND CANNOT REMAIN THE SAME.

Leader: Ask much from us,
expect much from us,
enable much by us,
encourage many through us.

ALL: SO, LORD, MAY WE LIVE TO YOUR GLORY,
BOTH AS INHABITANTS OF EARTH
AND CITIZENS OF THE COMMONWEALTH OF HEAVEN.
AMEN.

I waited on the Lord

Meditation 15

This script may be read simply by five people standing around the assembly with the Reader clearly visible to all or it may be dramatised as appropriate. An appropriate sung response to intersperse between the narrative is I WAITED ON THE LORD.

Ref: Lk.11:25–37

Personnel: **Victim**
Priest
Levite
Samaritan
Narrator

Victim: I waited on the Lord for five days.
I was at a festival,
a religious festival in a capital city.
It was seventeen miles from my home town,
seventeen miles of hills and rocks
and more hills and rocks.

ALL: *(Sung response)*
I WAITED, I WAITED ON THE LORD;
I WAITED, I WAITED ON THE LORD;
HE BENT DOWN LOW AND REMEMBERED ME
WHEN HE HEARD MY PRAYER.

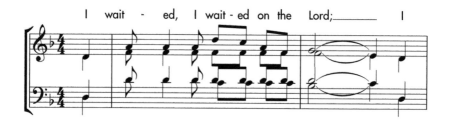

wait ed, I wait-ed on the Lord;_____ he bent down low and re-

mem - bered me when he heard my prayer.

Priest: I waited on the Lord.
I always do.
It's my job.
I'm a priest.
And I have a contract with my employer –
God –
that I don't get my hands dirty.

We have strict regulations
about what we can do,
and what we can handle …
nothing dead,
infectious or bloody.
I have to avoid getting contaminated.

ALL: *(Sung response)*

Levite: I waited on the Lord.
After all,
I am one of the Lord's humble servants,
not a priest …
but a Levite.
I teach the Law
from what you would call the Old Testament.
And sometimes I lead the prayers.

I live near the city where I work,
and I hurry home in case I get jumped.

ALL: *(Sung response)*

Samaritan: I waited on the Lord ...
in my own way.
I'm not a local,
not a priest,
not a teacher.
Priests and their like
would probably call me a heathen,
but they'd do that behind my back.
It would be against their principles
to speak to me face to face.

I'm just a traveller
with my own means of transport,
nothing fancy.

ALL: *(Sung response)*

Narrator: There was once a man
who was going down from Jerusalem to Jericho.

(The victim moves)

As he was travelling,
robbers attacked him,
stripped him
and beat him up,
leaving him half dead.

(The priest moves)

It so happened
that a priest was going down the same road.
He saw the man,
but walked by on the other side.

(The Levite moves)

After him a Levite came along.
He went over,
looked at the man,
and then walked on by,
on the other side.

(The Samaritan moves)

And then there was a Samaritan.
He was travelling the same way,
and when he came upon the man
and saw him,
his heart was filled with pity.

He went over to him,
poured wine and oil on his wounds
and bandaged them.

Then he took the man on his own animal.

(Samaritan helps the victim away)

He took him to an inn
and looked after him.

The next day he took out two silver coins
and gave them to the innkeeper,
saying,

Samaritan: *(From the distance)*
Take care of him
and when I come back,
I will pay you whatever else
you spend on him.

Lord Jesus, for you, money was not a dirty commodity

Prayer 13

Lord Jesus,
for you, money was not a dirty commodity,
the stuff of private conversations,
the enemy of all that is spiritual.

You handled coins,
paid taxes,
acknowledged the realities of trade and commerce,
and were unafraid to identify and condemn the misuse,
the false security and the lure of money.

Through your Holy Spirit,
inform the consciences of all who govern our finances,
fix trade prices,
raise interest rates
or cancel debt.

May money and morality never be kept poles apart
in national treasuries or private homes;
and though your head does not appear on our coinage,
may we use it as in your sight.
AMEN.

Not ... do you promise to be good

Prayer 14

This prayer may be used in association with the Gospel passage in which Jesus asks Peter, 'Do you love me?'

Ref: Jn.21:15–19

Not ... 'Do you promise to be good, Peter?'
Not ... 'Will you never let me down, Mary?'
Not ... 'Do you understand everything, Gordon?'
Not ... 'Will you never make a mistake, Sandra?'

Not even ... 'Can I trust you, Peter?'
but ... 'Do you love me?'
and 'Do you love me?'
and 'Do you love me?'

And to us ... whether we are long-time disciples,
          ... or just curious,
you come with the same question.

Because love is the rock
on which you build your church;
there is nothing stronger.

So, Jesus,
let us, with Peter, say,
          'Yes, Lord, you know that I love you,'
and then, with him,
follow you
today
and tomorrow
and for ever.
AMEN.

O Christ the Healer

Prayer 15

At the end of each petition, the Cantor begins the sung response LORD, IN YOUR MERCY HEAR OUR PRAYER. Alternatively, the text may be spoken.

Leader: Lord Jesus Christ,
greater than all things,
greater than every thought of you,
come, hear our prayer.

ALL: *(Sung or spoken response)*
LORD, IN YOUR MERCY,
HEAR OUR PRAYER

Leader: O Christ the Healer,
by your wounds others are made whole,
by your tears sorrow is washed away,
come with kindness
to those who today need your touch,
your time,
or who need to know that you remember them.

ALL: *(Sung or spoken response)*

Leader: O Christ the Feeder,
you ask for what we have
in order to nourish those we tend to forget.
Where people hunger,
in or out of the camera,
direct not just the pity of our eyes,
but our generosity even if it hurts.

ALL: *(Sung or spoken response)*

Leader: O Christ the Peacemaker,
stubbornness condemns us,
unsure as we are to walk the road that leads to peace.
Show us,
whose science is set to militarise the galaxy,
the simpler, humbler and yet more difficult path
by which our warfare may be turned to welfare.

ALL: *(Sung or spoken response)*

Leader: O Christ the Liberator,
the chains of death and hell could not hold you,
yet imperialism, racism, sexism
and a thousand other bogus ideologies
ensnare your people.
Where humanity cries out against inhumanity
and where Nature mourns for its lost good,
deliver all from evil.

ALL: *(Sung or spoken response)*

Leader: O Christ the Stranger,
you meet us when we are not ready for you;
you stand or sit with those we avoid;
you knock on the door we are hesitant to open;
you say the word we are reluctant to hear.
Come, where you are kept at arm's length
and take the hand that needs to hold you.

ALL: *(Sung or spoken response)*

Leader: Lord Jesus Christ,
we believe that you are God;
we believe that you are true to your promise
to answer the prayers of your people;

ALL: IN US,
THROUGH US,
AND, IF NEED BE, DESPITE US,
LET THE FABRIC OF THE WORLD
BE TRANSFORMED INTO THE SHAPE OF YOUR KINGDOM
FOR YOUR OWN NAME'S SAKE,
AMEN.

Of such is the kingdom
Script 15

This script or choral reading requires five solo voices and two choruses who pick up words already spoken by the others. Ideally all but the Jesus figure should be on the periphery of the congregation. Jesus, when the time comes for him to speak, should be in a position where he can see everyone.

At the end, the four main peripheral readers move towards Jesus and should have memorised the final words they say together.

A more complex reading of this script may involve percussive sounds being made under the main readers and between the main sections. It may also be possible to involve the readers plus Jesus in a simple circle dance action to conclude the piece.

Ref: Mk.3:1–6; Jn.8:1–11; Jn.9:1–41; Lk.8:40–42 & 49–56

Personnel: **A man**
A woman
A boy
A girl
Two choruses of voices
Jesus

Man: I,
I am,
I am the man,
I am the man with the withered arm,
the withered arm,
the withered arm.

Woman: I,
I am,
I am the woman,
I am the woman condemned by the crowd,
condemned by the crowd,
condemned by the crowd.

Boy: I,
I am,
I am the boy,
I am the boy who was sightless at birth,
sightless at birth,
sightless at birth.

Girl: I,
I am,
I am the girl,
I am the girl presumed to be dead,
presumed to be dead,
presumed to be dead.

Man: I am the man with the withered arm,
Chorus A: THE WITHERED ARM,
Chorus B: THE WITHERED ARM,
Man: who never intended to bother or harm
till I felt myself shaking with sudden alarm,
Chorus A: SUDDEN ALARM,
Chorus B: SUDDEN ALARM,
Man: when he asked me to move during worship.

Woman: I am the woman condemned by the crowd,
Chorus A: CONDEMNED BY THE CROWD,
Chorus B: CONDEMNED BY THE CROWD,
Woman: whose pleading for mercy was never allowed
till a man who I never knew scattered the proud,
Chorus A: SCATTERED THE PROUD,
Chorus B: SCATTERED THE PROUD,
Woman: as he knelt by my side and kept silent.

Boy: I am the boy who was sightless at birth,
Chorus A: SIGHTLESS AT BIRTH,
Chorus B: SIGHTLESS AT BIRTH,
Boy: the butt of cruel jokes
as my stick scraped the earth
till I silenced the noise of despicable mirth,
Chorus A: DESPICABLE MIRTH,
Chorus B: DESPICABLE MIRTH,
Boy: when he opened my eyes at the roadside.

Girl: I am the daughter presumed to be dead,
Chorus A: PRESUMED TO BE DEAD,
Chorus B: PRESUMED TO BE DEAD,

Girl: who no one believed would get up from her bed
               till they heard the request,
               'Please make sure that she's fed,'
Chorus A: MAKE SURE THAT SHE'S FED,
Chorus B: MAKE SURE THAT SHE'S FED,
Girl: when he called me to wake from my slumber.

Jesus: I … *(Looking around)*
               I …
               I …
               I did not come to lounge about
               with the leisured classes;
               I came to heal the sick.

               I did not come
               to patronise the wealthy;
               I came to preach the good news to the poor.

               I did not come
               to speak for the always articulate;
               I came to listen to the voiceless.
               I did not come
               to be shown what was wrong;
               I came to tell those who say,
               'We see, we see'
               that their clear vision
               is in fact blindness
               and their clear thinking
               is undermined by ignorance.

               I did not come
               to speak words of peace;
               I came to make signs of peace,
               knowing that the reconciliation God requires
               might cost me your friendship.

               I did not come
               to identify problems;
               I came to meet people,
               for people are always more important
               than their problems
               as life is always greater
               than its failures.

I did not come
to build a casualty clinic
and call it my church;
I came to announce God's kingdom
where all are taught and touched by each other,
where all are sisters and brothers of each other,
where justice and peace join hands
and conviction and commitment share the same lodging.

(Pause. He looks round)

And because,
and because,
and because,
and because the creatures of this earth seem convinced
that help comes from above
and scale the heights of fashion and intellect to find it ...
for that reason,
for that reason
I want you to know
that the love of God comes ...
from below
... in the child, *(Looks to the Girl who moves towards him)*
... in the stranger, *(Looks to the Man who moves)*
... in the wounded, *(Looks to the Boy who moves)*
... in the woman, *(Looks to the Woman who moves)*

*(When the four speakers are in proximity to each other, they
face the congregation and join their hands and speak together
slowly)*

ALL:	We are the people whom no one would touch,
Chorus A:	NO ONE WOULD TOUCH,
Chorus B:	NO ONE WOULD TOUCH,
ALL:	the poor of the world who were never loved much
	till a voice from among us declared
	that of such,
Chorus A:	OF SUCH,
Chorus B:	OF SUCH,
Jesus:	*(Joining hands amidst the others)*
	... of such is the kingdom of heaven.

The adulteress
Reading 10

This monologue may be used individually as a comment on the Gospel reading, or together with those on pages 213, 216 & 222, following each other as an extended meditation on the range of people whom Jesus healed.

Ref: Jn.8:1–11

I wasn't ill.

Oh there were rumours.
I knew about them before
and I heard about them afterwards.

I was supposed to have given syphilis to half the men in the village.
I was rumoured to be the cause of two women
giving birth to deaf children.
People thought that my door was open night and day
to every drunk or lecher looking for a good time.

The phrase people would use was:
'He must have been with Annie.'

If an apprentice arrived late and bleary-eyed for work
one of the older men would say,
'Were you with Annie last night?'

If somebody started scratching their head or their groin,
somebody else would suggest, 'Looks as if you've been with Annie.'

But none of them had ever 'been' with me.

My reputation developed because I had twins out of wedlock.
I gave my virginity to a man who said he'd marry me.
Two days later he got drowned at sea.

And because he came from a decent family,
and because I loved him,
I never told anyone that he was the father of my boys.

I suppose if there had been just one child, it would have been easier.

But because there were two, the gossips had a field day,
saying that Samuel, the older by an hour,
looked like John Jacobson the timber merchant
while Matthew, the younger,
looked like Gary Mitchell, the undertaker.

I had to put up with this for ten years,
and I had never retaliated,
and I had never given myself to another man …

… until one day … and I don't know why,
I let myself be swept off my feet by a married man
who said that his wife couldn't understand him.

I gave him my sympathy,
I gave him my time.
But I never thought that it would go further than friendship;
and I had no idea that his wife was watching every move.

She chose her time well,
and she brought eight or maybe nine men with her
who wanted to have their fantasies confirmed.

They called me a slut, a whore, a filthy bitch;
they dragged me by the hair through the streets
into the village square.

Old men prodded me with their sticks,
young men tramped on my fingers;
women spat.

At six o'clock they were going to stone me.

At ten to six, he knelt down beside me,
and whatever he said to them, they disappeared.

And when he said to me, 'I forgive you,'
I knew that I was healed …
even though I had never been ill.

The day of judgement
Meditation 16

For this meditation, the Reader, Jesus and voices A and B should be located at the four main points of the compass, with Jesus opposite the Reader. Voice C sits in the midst of the assembly. Names should be freely changed to suit local circumstances and world news.

Ref: Matt.25:31–46

Personnel: **Reader**
          A
          B
          C
          Jesus

Reader: When the Son of Man comes in his glory
and all the angels with him,
he will sit on his royal throne
and the people of all nations …

A: Scotland,

B: Serbia,

A: England,

B: India,

A: Ireland,

B: Iraq,

A: Wales,

B: Botswana …

Reader: … and the people of all nations
will be gathered before him.

Then he will divide them into two groups,
as a shepherd separates sheep from goats.

He will put the righteous people on his right
and the others on his left.

Then the king will say to those on his right,

Jesus: Come and possess the kingdom
which has been prepared for you
before the world began.

Reader: And when they ask him why,
he will tell them
that whatever they did
to the least of his brothers and sisters,
they did to him.

Then he will say to those on his left,

Jesus: Get away from me!
You are under God's curse!
Away to the eternal fire
prepared for the devil and his angels!

For I was hungry ...

A: in Mogadishu,

B: in Manchester,

A: in Calcutta,

B: in Castlemilk,

Jesus: but you would not feed me.

I was thirsty ...

A: for water in the Sudan,

B: for company in London,

A: for change in China,

B: for justice in Somalia,

Jesus: but you not would quench my thirst.

I was a stranger …

A: a Catholic in the Falls Road,

B: a Palestinian in Beirut,

A: a Mozambiquan in Malawi,

B: a Bangladeshi in Tower Hamlets,

Jesus: … but you would not take me into your home.

I was naked …

A: among the street children in Rio,

B: among the desolate in Rwanda,

A: among the homeless in Haiti,

B: among the hopeless in Harare,

Jesus: … but you would not clothe me.

I was sick …

A: dying of Aids in Uganda,

B: crippled with arthritis in the Southern General,

A: waiting for medicine in Siberia,

B: recovering from alchoholism in Leverndale,

Jesus: … but you would not take care of me.

I was in prison …

A: in Peterhead,

B: on Robben Island,

A: in Cornton Vale,

B: in Alcatraz,

Jesus: … and you would not visit me.

Reader: And when they answer,

C: Lord, when did we see you and never help you?

Reader: … the King will reply,

Jesus: Whenever you refused
to help the least important people …

A: the cardboard city people,

B: the 'discharged-into-the-community' people,

A: the asylum seekers,

B: the mentally handicapped,

Jesus: … whenever you refused to help them,
you refused to help me.

Reader: And this will happen on the day when,
before his throne,
the Son of Man will gather together
all nations like

A: Scotland,

B: Serbia,

A: England,

B: India,

A: Ireland,

B: Iraq,

A: Wales,

B: Botswana.

The haemorrhaging woman
Reading 11

*This and the monologues on pages 207, 216 and 222 may either be used indi-
vidually as a comment on the relevant Gospel reading, or they may follow each
other as an extended meditation on the range of people whom Jesus healed. In
the latter instance, it would be important to sing a chant such as I WAITED ON
THE LORD (from ENEMY OF APATHY) or DON'T BE AFRAID (from COME ALL
YOU PEOPLE) before and after each monologue.*

*Readers should be chosen not for their erudition, but for the earthiness of their
voices. While there is no requirement that the texts should be memorised, the
more the reader is at home with and inside the text, the more convincing will
the reading be as a testimony.*

*Depending on locality, it may be necessary to change particular words in the
text (e.g. the names of songs or types of confectionery) to suit the prevalent
culture.*

Ref: Lk.8:43–48

Now, don't you get me wrong – for everyone else does.

I am not a quiet wee (*little*) mouse
and I never have been.

With a name like 'Big Isa'
I could hardly ever have been petite.

I was always in the limelight.
I always chased the boys before they chased me,
and if ever there was a ceilidh or a karaoke night
I'd be there singing 'I Did It My Way'
or 'Who's Sorry Now?' at the drop of a hat.

I used to be 23 stone (*320 pounds*) …
though many of these weren't stones (*pounds*) at all
but clotted cream caramels, sherbet bon-bons
and chocolate eclairs.

I was 36 when the bleeding started.
But of course, it was never called 'bleeding'.
It was a 'discharge' according to the doctor;
just another aspect of 'women's troubles'.

'Listen, doctor' I says,
'the only trouble that we women have is men like you!
I'm not "discharging".
What do you think I am … A sewage pipe?
And I don't have "women's troubles".
I must be losing something like a pint of blood a week.'

Well, the doctor said there was nothing for it.

So I tried other options:
copper bangles,
a rabbit's paw under my pillow,
bathing in salt water when there was a full moon.

I went on a seven-day silent retreat.
I paid three weeks' wages to some Italian gigolo
for crystals which he said
had healed half the folk in Rome.

And all the time I was losing weight …
and losing hope.

'Big Isa' became 'Isa'
and then 'Wee (*little*) Isa'.

And then I heard that he was coming to our village.
It was my last chance and I knew it.

I thought I might just squeeze through the crowd,
but that was useless.
They were tight packed round him like sardines.

So, where I got the strength from I don't know,
but I just got in there.

I shoved, I pulled,
I kicked an old man in the shins;
I bit somebody in the arm
who tried to keep me back.

And then …
then I saw him,
and I said,
'God … this time … please!'
And I threw myself forward
and just managed to touch his sleeve
before some odd man
who smelt of fish gave me such a shove
that I fell on my backside.

But that was enough.
It worked …
though I was a quivering wreck when I realised
that the whole procession had stopped
and everybody was looking in my direction.

He said that it was my faith that did it.
But I had had faith before …
in the doctor …
in the crystals.

It wasn't just my faith.
It was him.

The leper
Reading 12

This monologue may be used individually as a comment on the Gospel reading, or together with those on pages 207, 213 & 222, following each other as an extended meditation on the range of people whom Jesus healed.

Ref: Lk.17:11–19

You should have seen the priest's face
when I arrived at the door.
I suppose me grinning all over didn't exactly help.

He knew my family ... especially my father
who had helped to build the parish hall.
My dad and the priest were very close,
but they never talked about me.

You see, when you get leprosy
you don't belong any more.
You don't belong to your family;
you don't belong in the church.

This was the priest
who had confirmed the diagnosis,
the priest who had sent me from the sanctuary,
never to return,
asking God to 'have mercy' on my soul ...
the kind of thing you'd say
to a criminal en route to the gallows.

But here I was back ...
seven years later,
minus an arm,
presenting myself as cured.

He didn't know what to say.
He didn't know which book to look for
or which page to turn.

He had only been taught the ceremonial word
with which to send lepers away.
He had never learned
how to receive them back.

It took a long while,
a long while for him to come
within three feet (*a metre*) of me.

He wanted me to tie a blindfold on
until I said,
'I've only got one arm.
You'll have to do it.'

But he couldn't bring himself to touch me.
So he asked me to put a sack over my head,
and then he took a pin
and began to stick it
into different parts of my body
saying, 'Where am I touching?'

And every time I knew;
because every time it hurt.
Pain had returned because I was healthy.

He even pushed the pin into my stump
and I yelled.
Actually I yelled louder than I needed to,
but I reckoned that if this guy
was going to give me a hard time,
he should feel some of the pain too.

Then he took the bag off my head
and said …
'How is this possible?'

I said,
'It's possible
because in a world where everybody,
including my religious friends,
has kept back and avoided me,
somebody …
one man …
touched me.

No, he didn't just touch me,
he embraced me
as if I were the lost brother
he'd always wanted to find.'

The priest didn't ask his name.
It was as if he knew,
and as if he were disappointed
that what religion turned away from
God embraced.

↑ The log in your eye
Symbolic action 2

This script requires, for the symbolic action, an open area in the middle of the assembly. In the centre there should be low tables about 18 inches off the ground, covered entirely with mirrors laid horizontally. The mirrors in turn are covered with small blocks of wood. These can be a range of different sizes, and there should be at least as many blocks as there are worshippers.

The height of the mirrors and that they are completely covered by the blocks is crucial, so that as the blocks are removed people see their reflection in that segment of revealed mirror.

Ref: Matt.7:1–5; Lk.6:37–42

Leader: Towards the end of the meditation,
we may, if we wish,
come slowly to the table,
lift a small piece of wood from the mirror
in order to see more of our faces,
and leave it at the side.

For the first part of the meditation,
it may feel best to close our eyes.

(Pause)

Imagine entering a room,
with chairs round the wall
and dim lighting,
and silence.

You find a seat,
and sit down,
and as you look around,
you discover that your vision is blurred.

You cannot see clearly
the people who sit around you
and you cannot see clearly
the table in the middle of the floor
around which everyone is sitting.

And you are thinking
'What's wrong with my eyes?'

You hear the voices of those around you.

They are the voices of people
who are telling each other the truth ...
about themselves,
about their past hurts,
about their secret hopes,
about their faith and their doubts.

And each voice you recognise,
even though you can see no face,
because each voice belongs to someone
whom you have judged and found wanting.

Each voice belongs to someone
who has been ignored,
or chastised,
or gossiped about
or put down in conversation
because you knew only part of their story .

And now you hear it all.

And as they speak,
their voices summon up the emotions
which led you to make judgement:
your impatience with people
        who take a long time to say what they mean,
your jealousy of those
        who do what you wish you could do
        or have what you wish you could have,
your anger at those
        who hold opinions which you cannot agree with,
your fear of those
        whose generosity or thoughtfulness
        shows up your own indifference.

And as you listen,
as you are compelled to listen
to what is in their hearts,
and realise what is in yours,
as you bow your head
and regret all the quick conclusions
and false presumptions,
someone sits down on the seat beside you.

Without warning the voice says,
'Can you see?'

And, shaking your head, you say,
'No … no one … nothing …'

And then the voice says,
'You've got a log in your eye,
 and until you get rid of that,
 you'll never see yourself,
 or your neighbour,
 or your God.'

And then this unnamed stranger walks
towards the table in the middle of the room,
inviting you to follow …
and do something
about the log in your eye.

(Music, during which people move to lift a wooden block from the mirror. A prayer may follow.)

The paralysed man at the pool
Reading 13

This monologue may be used individually as a comment on the Gospel reading, or together with those on pages 207, 213 & 216, following each other as an extended meditation on the range of people whom Jesus healed.

Ref: Jn.5:1–18

The thing to remember about me
is that I had no idea who he was.

I contracted polio when I was about six,
and there was nothing that could be done.
So, when I was twelve,
my father took me to the pool.

Other boys got a barmitzvah;
I got taken to a shrine …
well it wasn't really a shrine …
there was this thing about how if the water moved
the first person in got cured.

Listen, I lay there for 38 years
and there were no cures,
just a lot of speculation.

I suppose you might say that I got comfortable there.
I mean, I might have been a cripple
but I could talk and laugh.
I said hello to everybody by name
and it paid dividends –
people put money into my hat.

It wasn't the best existence,
but it wasn't the worst.

And then one day up comes this total stranger.
Now when I say 'total' I mean 'total'.
I never knew him, he never knew me.

He didn't ask who I was or tell me his name.
He just said,
'Do you want to get better?'

I felt like saying,
'Do you think I've been lying on this stretcher for forty years
just to get a sun tan?'

But I didn't.
I didn't like his question.
It threatened me.
To get better would mean becoming responsible.
To get better would mean walking and working
and putting money into other beggars' hats.

In fact, I nearly said, 'Leave me alone.'

But there was something in his directness,
something in the way he cut across forty years of apathy.

So I said yes.
And ever since, I've been standing on my feet
in more ways than one.

But I didn't know him.
And when the thought police began to ask questions
about who had cured me, I couldn't give a name.

All I could say was,
'The man who asked awkward questions.'

Through our lives

Prayer 16

Leader: Let us pray.

Lord God,
in Jesus, you came in the body:
flesh of our flesh, bone of our bone,
one with us in searing pain and delirious laughter.

We thank you that you did not remain an idea,
even a religious idea,
but walked, wept and washed feet among us.

By your love,
change our ideas,
especially our religious ideas,
into living signs of your worth and will.

ALL: THROUGH OUR LIVES AND BY OUR PRAYERS,
YOUR KINGDOM COME.

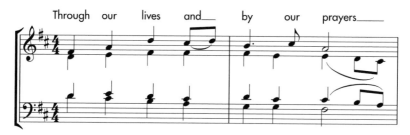

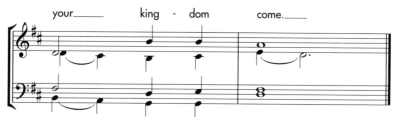

Leader: Lord God,
in Jesus, you touched the scabby (*suffering*),
listened to the ignored,
gave the depressed something to hope for.
You bandaged the broken with love
and healed them.

We believe that your power to heal
is still present,
so on your help we call, remembering
those whose minds are menaced by thoughts
    which worry or wound them,
those whose hearts are broken because love has gone
    or because the light they lived by
    has turned to darkness,
those whose feet walk in circles,
    stopping only when they are tired,
    resting only to walk in circles again,
those whose flesh and bone or mind and spirit
    are filled with pain,
those who feel discarded or disposable.

O Christ put your hands where our prayers beckon.

(Silence)

ALL: THROUGH OUR LIVES AND BY OUR PRAYERS,
YOUR KINGDOM COME.

Leader: Lord God,
in Jesus, your body was broken
by the cowardly and powerful.
The judgement hall of Pilate
knew your silence
as surely as your critics knew your voice.

In word and silence,
take on the powerful of the world today:
those whose word sentences some to cruelty
    or unmerited redundancy;
those whose word transfers wealth or weapons
    for the sake of profit or prejudice;
those whose silence condones the injustice
    they have the power to change.

O Saviour of the poor, liberate your people.

(Silence)

ALL: THROUGH OUR LIVES AND BY OUR PRAYERS,
YOUR KINGDOM COME.

Leader: Lord God,
by the authority of scripture,
we learn that we are the body of Christ …
yes, even we who worship in different ways,
even we whose understanding of you
is so changeable,
even we who, in our low moments,
make an idol of our insignificance.

We are your body, we are told.

Then, Lord,
make us like you
that our souls may be the stained glass
through which your light and purpose
bring beauty into the world.

(Silence)

ALL: THROUGH OUR LIVES AND BY OUR PRAYERS,
YOUR KINGDOM COME.

Leader: Your kingdom come,
in joy and generosity,
in the small and the large,
the ordinary and the special,
and to you be the glory
now and always.
ALL: AMEN.

Unclean, unclean!
Script 16

Reader A stands at the lectern and his/her Assistant is nearby. The other characters should be dotted around the audience/congregation.

After each has been 'condemned' or during their condemnation, the Assistant should, at the behest of Reader A, put some mark on them or do some action which singles them out from the others. It may be that they physically leave the hall, returning only at the second part of the script. After the removal of the 'condemned', Reader A should leave the lectern. A short silence or piece of music may ensue. Then Reader B goes to the lectern. The five 'condemned' stand at the back to make their common response in unison.

After this script, it is very easy to enable an assembly to reflect together on the implications of Jesus' ministry of healing and reconciliation.

Ref: Lev.13:1ff; Lk.17:11–19

Personnel: **Reader A**, *who is also the Priest*
Assistant
Alec McCowan, *who is HIV-positive*
Mary Jenkins, *an unmarried mother*
Irene Jamieson, *an ex-convict*
Ashok Ashley, *a man of mixed race*
Hugh Wetherburn, *an unemployed worker*
Reader B

Part 1

Reader A: This is the law of Moses.
It is found in the book of Leviticus, chapter 13.
It concerns leprosy.

(Reader A reads as from Bible)

If anyone has a sore on his skin
or a boil or an inflammation
which could develop into leprosy,
he shall be brought to the priest.

The priest shall examine him,
and if it is discovered
that the disease is deeper
than the surrounding skin,
the priest shall pronounce that person unclean.

If the disorder does not appear
to be any more than skin deep,
the priest shall isolate the person for seven days.

Then on the seventh day,
he will examine the person again.
And if he examines him
and finds that the disease has spread,
he shall pronounce the person unclean.

And as long as the disease prevails,
the person must live away from the community,
away from all the others.

(Reader A closes Bible)

… and I am the priest
and am charged with the responsibility
of keeping this community healthy,
and of declaring unclean
those whose presence is a threat
to the health of all the others.

And I have made examination of you all,
and have examined my conscience
and now must pronounce the verdict
which it is my right and duty to administer.

(Reader A looks round)

Alec McCowan.

Alec: Yes.

Reader A: Have you had the results of your blood test?

Alec: No.

Reader A: Think again.
I spoke to your consultant on Thursday.

	Well?
Alec:	OK. They came yesterday.
Reader A:	And?
Alec:	I've been scared to open the envelope.
Reader A:	Shall I tell you what it says?
Alec:	No ... no.
Reader A:	But I will. I have to. I have to tell you and everyone else ... It was positive.
Alec:	*(Shouts)* No!
Reader A:	It was positive. It was HIV positive. That means you're a carrier. A carrier of Acquired Immune Deficiency Syndrome ... AIDS. That means that you are a threat to everyone around you. I have to protect people from you and from the likes of you, Mr McCowan. I have to pronounce you unclean. *(The agreed action happens)*
Reader A:	Mary Jenkins.
Mary:	Yes ...
Reader A:	You've had a test done too, Mary, haven't you?
Mary:	Yes, but I've not got AIDS.
Reader A:	No, but your test was positive too, wasn't it?
Mary:	Yes ... How did you know?

Reader A: That doesn't matter.
What matters is that your test was positive …
your pregnancy test.

People around you looked shocked …
a decent girl like you.

Who's the father, Mary?
Is he here?

(No answer)

Is he here or are you trying to protect him?

(No answer)

No answer …
Mary, you've caused heartbreak to your mother,
and a disgrace to your family.
You've set an example
we don't want others to copy.
I've no option …
but to say …
that you are unclean and unwanted.

(Agreed action)

Reader A: Irene Jamieson …

Irene: I'm no' pregnant!

Reader A: No.

Irene: And I've no' got AIDS!

Reader A: It's hardly likely
that you could be pregnant or get AIDS
where you've been this past three years.
Is it?

Where have you been, Irene?
Tell everybody …

Irene: Stirling.
(Here, the name of a local town or city housing a women's prison should be substituted)

230

Reader A: Which part of Stirling, Irene?

Irene: Cornton …

Reader A: Cornton *Vale*.
Cornton …
Vale …
Prison.

And you were there
because you ran a racket selling dope.

And when you couldn't get junkies
to buy your smash,
you sold your body,
because you needed money to feed your habit.

Irene: But that's in the past.
I've done time.

Reader A: Yes … you've done time.
But I'm thinking about the present.

I'm thinking
of what you might be tempted to do again.
I'm thinking of all the damage you could do
if you were tempted.

It's for your own good.
It's for the common good.

(Agreed action)

Ashok Ashley.

(He stands)

… or should it be Ashok Mohammed?

Ashok: Ashok Ashley.

Reader A: Your mother's name?
Why not your father's name?

Ashok: He doesn't live with us.

Reader A: That's right
But he is your father.
Are you not proud of your father?

Ashok: I see him from time to time.

Reader A: I didn't ask you if you saw him.
I asked you if you were proud of him.

Ashok ...
you are half-Scottish and half-Indian,
(Substitute racial groups as necessary)
half-white and half-brown.

But your presence here makes things difficult.
You know that.
You get called a wog or a Paki.
You get slogans painted on your door.

Ashok: I can't help that!

Reader A: No. But the neighbours don't like it.
They want to live in peace.
They don't want drunk boys
hanging about the door at midnight,
shouting 'Go home, darkie!'

You'll have to move ...
for their good ...
for your own good ...
for our good ...

(Agreed action)

Reader A: Hugh Wetherburn.

Hugh: Uh huh?

Reader A: Did you go to the restart interview on Wednesday, Hugh?

Hugh: Yes.

Reader A: What did they say?

Hugh: The same as they said before.
They don't have any jobs for mechanics in the area.

Reader A: To be more precise, Hugh …
they don't have any jobs for *tank* mechanics.

Hugh: Yes, but the army said
that I could use my trade anywhere.

Reader A: The army will tell you anything
to get you in.

But when you come out, you find, Hugh,
that there are very few people
who want the steering adjusted on their Chieftain tank.

Very few people
who want a Bailey bridge slung across the burn (*stream*)
at the bottom of their garden …

Very few people
who need somebody
who's trained to listen in to the signals
the Russians are sending to their submarines.

How long have you been unemployed?

Hugh: Three years.

Reader A: You know, Hugh …
unemployment is a disease.
In this neighbourhood,
it has reached epidemic proportions.

And you know what happens when you have an epidemic?
You isolate people.
You send them away to where they might get better.
… or in your case where they might get a job.

Hugh: But I was born and bred here!

Reader A: But there's no work for you here.
You've just become a parasite …
a social leper.

I've no option …

(*Agreed action*)

Part 2

Reader B: As Jesus made his way to Jerusalem,
he went along
between the border of Samaria and Galilee.

He was going into a village
where he met ten men
suffering from leprosy.
They stood at a distance and shouted,

ALL: *(From the wings)*
'JESUS, MASTER, TAKE PITY ON US.'

Reader B: Jesus saw them and said to them,

'Go and let the priests examine you.'

On the way they were made clean.
When one of them saw that he was healed,
he came back praising God in a loud voice.

He threw himself on the ground at Jesus' feet
and thanked him.

The man was a Samaritan.

Jesus said,
'There were ten men who were healed;
where are the other nine?

Why is this foreigner the only one
who came back to give thanks to God?'

And Jesus said to him,
'Get up, your faith has made you well.'

You came to bring health

Prayer 17

During this prayer the response LORD, TO WHOM SHALL WE GO? may be sung.

Ref: Jn.6:60–71

Leader: Lord Jesus,
you came to bring health.

You said,
'I have come
that you might have life in its fullness.'

We trust what you said
and entrust to you
those who we know need healing
and those not known to us
whose research, skill or prayers bring health.

ALL: LORD, TO WHOM SHALL WE GO?
YOURS ARE THE WORDS OF ETERNAL LIFE.

Leader: Lord Jesus,
you came to bring peace.

You said,
'Blessed are the peacemakers,
they shall be called the children of God.'

We trust what you said
and entrust to you
those who want and work for peace.

ALL: (Sung response)

Leader: Lord Jesus,
you came to bring people value.

You said,
'The last shall be first;
the least are as good as the greatest.'

We trust what you said
and entrust to you
those who have no work,
no sense of worth,
who need to know that they are wanted.

ALL: (Sung response)

Leader: Lord Jesus,
you came to bring reconciliation.

In you there is neither Jew nor Gentile,
neither black nor white.

We trust you
and entrust to you
those whose lives are battered by prejudice
and those who try to join hands
separated by hate.

ALL: (Sung response)

Leader: Lord Jesus,
you came to feed the world.

You said,
'I am the bread of life.'

We trust you
and we entrust to you
those who starve
and those who work to move the minds of the overfed
and to empty their wallets.

ALL: *(Sung response)*

Leader: Lord Jesus,
you came to build your church.

You said to us,
'You are the salt of the earth.
You are light for all the world.'

Say these words again,
quietly or loudly,
until, with you,
we become agents of God's liberation.

ALL: AMEN.

Sources of suggested songs, chants and sung responses

ADORAMUS TE, DOMINE Taizé Community
Songs and prayers from Taizé (Geoffrey Chapman/Mowbray, 1991)
ALLELUIA (various)
Come all you people (Wild Goose Publications, 1995)
There is one among us (Wild Goose Publications, 1998)
BEHOLD THE LAMB OF GOD John L. Bell
Come all you people (Wild Goose Publications, 1995)
DON'T BE AFRAID John L. Bell
Come all you people (Wild Goose Publications, 1995)
HE HAD NO WIFE/THE FAMILY John L. Bell
Love & anger (Wild Goose Publications, 1997)
JESUS CHRIST, SON OF GOD AMONG US John L. Bell;
There is one among us (Wild Goose Publications, 1998)
KINDLE A FLAME TO LIGHTEN THE DARK John L. Bell & Graham Maule
Heaven shall not wait (Wild Goose Publications, 1989)
KYRIE ELEISON
Many & great (Wild Goose Publications, 1990)
Come all you people (Wild Goose Publications, 1995)
There is one among us (Wild Goose Publications, 1998)
OH LORD, HEAR MY PRAYER Taizé Community;
Songs and prayers from Taizé (Geoffrey Chapman/Mowbray, 1991)
Common ground (St Andrew Press, 1998)
OVER MY HEAD African American traditional
Love & anger (Wild Goose Publications, 1997)
POWER John L. Bell & Graham Maule
Heaven shall not wait (Wild Goose Publications, 1989)
THE SON OF MARY John L. Bell & Graham Maule
Heaven shall not wait (Wild Goose Publications, 1989)
THE SONG OF THE CROWD John L. Bell & Graham Maule
Heaven shall not wait (Wild Goose Publications, 1989)
UBI CARITAS Taizé Community
Songs and prayers from Taizé (Geoffrey Chapman/Mowbray, 1991)
WATCH AND PRAY John L. Bell & Graham Maule
Enemy of apathy (Wild Goose Publications, 1988)
WHO AM I? John L. Bell & Graham Maule
Enemy of apathy (Wild Goose Publications, 1988)
YOUR KINGDOM COME, O LORD Prof. Nikolai Zabolotski
Many & great (Wild Goose Publications, 1990)

Index of biblical references

Index of first lines

189 – Jesus stood up to read and the scroll of the prophet Isaiah was given to him / **Narrator**

99 – Jesus went away to the countryside near the city of Tyre / **Narrator**

76 – Let us remember and celebrate twelve of Jesus' disciples / **A**

85 – Look at your hands. See the touch and the tenderness / **Leader**

224 – Lord God, in Jesus, you came in the body / **Leader**

200 – Lord Jesus Christ, greater than all things … / **Leader**

198 – Lord Jesus, for you, money was not a dirty commodity / **Leader**

86 – Lord Jesus, when you took a child and told adults to become like her / **Leader**

235 – Lord Jesus, you came to bring health / **Leader**

199 – Not … 'Do you promise to be good, Peter?' / **Leader**

213 – Now, don't you get me wrong – for everyone else does / **Haemorrhaging woman**

41 – Power stalks the earth both by purpose and accident / **Reader**

104 – Save us, Lord, from the temptation to buy what we do not need / **Leader**

57 – So …; So …; So …; So …; / **Peter; James; Peter; John**

117 – So, you say you saw her / **Detective**

110 – Steal, Jesus, steal from us the grudge we will not let go / **Reader**

42 – That we worship one God, Creator, Christ and Holy Spirit / **Leader**

222 – The thing to remember about me is that I had no idea who he was / **Paralytic at the pool**

174 – There was once a rich woman who dressed in expensive clothes / **Narrator**

134 – They were sitting on the ground, four of them / **Reader**

93 – This is a prayer which Jesus heard, 'Lord, have mercy on me … a sinner' / **Leader**

165 – This is a story of Jesus: a sower went out to sow … / **Narrator**

227 – This is the law of Moses / **Reader A**

53 – To him who walks among the crowds / **Reader**

136 – Today we remember, Lord, those who have yet to throw in their lot with you / **Leader**

219 – Towards the end of the meditation, we may … come slowly to the table/ **Leader**

21 – Watched by shepherds, he is lying in wool / **A**

111 – When I was a child, I gave him all I had / **A**

19 – When the lights are on and the house is full / **Leader**

209 – When the son of man comes in his glory / **Reader**

60 – Who am I? Not the one you choose / **Reader**

65 – You are the unseen guest at every table / **Leader**

153 – You broke down the barriers when you crept in beside us / **Leader**

216 – You should have seen the priest's face / **Leper**

The Wild Goose Resource & Worship Groups

The **Wild Goose Resource Group** is an expression of the Iona Community's commitment to the renewal of public worship. Based in Glasgow, the Group has four members (Alison Adam, John Bell, Graham Maule and Mairi Munro) who are employed full-time and who lead workshops and seminars throughout Britain and abroad.

From 1984 to 2001, the four WGRG workers were also part of the **Wild Goose Worship Group**. The WGWG consisted of around sixteen, predominantly lay, people at any one time, who came from a variety of occupational and denominational backgrounds. Over the 17 years of its existence, it was the WGWG who tested, as well as promoted, the material in this book.

The task of both groups has been to develop and identify new methods and materials to enable the revitalisation of congregational song, prayer and liturgy. The songs and liturgical material have now been translated and used in many countries across the world as well as being frequently broadcast on radio and television.

The WGRG publishes a twice-yearly newsletter, **GOOSEgander**, to enable friends and supporters to keep abreast of WGRG developments. If you would like to receive GOOSEgander, please copy and complete the form overleaf.

The Iona Community

The Iona Community, founded in 1938 by the Revd George MacLeod, then a parish minister in Glasgow, is an ecumenical Christian community committed to seeking new ways of living the Gospel in today's world. Initially working to restore part of the medieval abbey on Iona, the Community today remains committed to 'rebuilding the common life' through working for social and political change, striving for the renewal of the church with an ecumenical emphasis, and exploring new, more inclusive approaches to worship, all based on an integrated understanding of spirituality.

The Community now has over 240 Members, about 1500 Associate Members and around 1500 Friends. The Members – women and men from many denominations and backgrounds (lay and ordained), living throughout Britain with a few overseas – are committed to a fivefold Rule of devotional discipline, sharing and accounting for use of time and money, regular meeting, and action for justice and peace.

At the Community's three residential centres – the Abbey and the MacLeod Centre on Iona, and Camas Adventure Camp on the Ross of Mull – guests are welcomed from March to October and over Christmas. Hospitality is provided for over 110 people, along with a unique opportunity, usually through week-long programmes, to extend horizons and forge relationships through sharing an experience of the common life in worship, work, discussion and relaxation. The Community's shop on Iona, just outside the Abbey grounds, carries an attractive range of books and craft goods.

The Community's administrative headquarters are in Glasgow, which also serves as a base for its work with young people, the Wild Goose Resource Group working in the field of worship, a bi-monthly magazine, *Coracle*, and a publishing house, Wild Goose Publications.

For information on the Iona Community contact:
The Iona Community
Fourth Floor, Savoy House,
140 Sauchiehall Street, Glasgow G2 3DH, UK
Phone: 0141 332 6343
e-mail: ionacomm@gla.iona.org.uk   web: www.iona.org.uk

For enquiries about visiting Iona, please contact:
Iona Abbey
Isle of Iona
Argyll PA76 6SN, UK
Phone: 01681 700404   e-mail: ionacomm@iona.org.uk

More titles from the Wild Goose Resource Group

CLOTH FOR THE CRADLE
Worship resources and readings for Advent, Christmas and Epiphany
Wild Goose Worship Group

The first of the series of which *Present on Earth* is part, this rediscovery of the stories of Christ's birth through adult eyes contains much to reflect on individually and to use in group and worship situations. The material is drawn from the work of the Wild Goose Resource and Worship Groups whose innovative style of worship is widely admired and imitated.

G-5109 • 150 pp

STAGES ON THE WAY
Worship Resources for Lent, Holy Week and Easter
Wild Goose Worship Group

The second of this series of three collections of resources, this 'book of bits' for worship produced by the Wild Goose Worship Group has been received with great enthusiasm by clergy and laity alike. Tracing Jesus' road to the cross through Lent, Holy Week and Easter, its prime purpose is to resource worship that enables people to sense the hope, apprehension and joy of Easter as felt by Jesus' friends. The range and diversity offers a unique source of elements for lay and clergy worship planners and enablers.

G-5110 • 240 pp

JESUS AND PETER
Off-the-record conversations
John L Bell & Graham Maule

A revised and expanded edition of John L. Bell and Graham Maule's much-loved unrecorded dialogues between Jesus and his eager disciple, Peter – perfect as discussion starters, scriptural reflections in small groups and church services, or for personal study. In true Wild Goose Resource Group tradition, these scripts use completely up-to-date language and present a dynamic modern perspective on perennial issues such as faith, money, marriage, vocation, sex, healing, taxes, ecological concern, commitment, children, the kingdom of heaven, and much more.

G-5288 • 128 pp

HE WAS IN THE WORLD
Meditations for public worship
John L Bell

Twenty-five meditations with notes suggesting appropriate ways of using the material.
Pastoral: The starfish ● The clown ● The teachers ● I never wanted to be born ● Fourspeak *Personal:* The rabbit hutch ● Pethla ● On the bus ● The cupboard ● Writing it down ● The saints of God *Biblical:* When the time was right ● On the eighth day ● Meeting God ● He was in the world ● Behold the Lamb of God ● The testimony and prayers of three anonymous children ● Lazarus ● The tree ● We did not want to go ● The stranger ● Three stone meditations ● God's own people

G-4393 • 104 pp

STATES OF BLISS AND YEARNING
The marks and means of authentic Christian spirituality
John L Bell

Spirituality is not a permanent high, a continual blissed-out state. To experience the heights, one has also to know the depths. In this book based on speeches and sermons delivered in marquees, cathedrals and local churches, John Bell deals with issues as diverse as private devotion and public debt. The picture of God that emerges is not one of a 'celestial sadist' but rather a compassionate being who asks that we do only what we can, starting from where we are, to be just and compassionate too.

G-5769 • 112 pp

COME ALL YOU PEOPLE
Shorter songs for worship sung by the Wild Goose Worship Group
Songbook/cassette/CD
John L Bell

Forty-seven chants, responses, choruses, introits and shorter songs are featured in the songbook. The cassette contains twenty-one of the songs and demonstrates imaginative ways to use the material. Sources of inspiration for these songs are Southern Africa, the Russian Orthodox Church, Charismatic assemblies in Central and Southern America and ancient Scottish church traditions.

G-4391 Music Collection • 96 pp
CD-355 Compact Disc • CS-355 Cassette

THERE IS ONE AMONG US

Shorter songs for worship
Songbook/cassette/CD
Wild Goose Worship Group

Simple yet richly rewarding wee songs from the popular Wild Goose Worship Group which can be used in a variety of situations from cathedrals to classrooms, open air festivals to in-house groups. Excellent for innovative and participatory styles of worship. The songbook also gives helpful hints on using the material and includes an appendix of new readings and prayers for use with the songs.

CD/cassette playlist:
SIDE ONE: *Gathering:* Alleluia, Bless the Lord; *Penitence:* Kyrie Eleison, Lo, I am with you; *Scripture:* Magnificat, First born of Mary; *Concern:* Lord, in your mercy; *Eucharist:* O Lamb of God, This is the body of Christ; *Leaving:* Jesus Christ, Ameni.
SIDE TWO: *Gathering:* Give thanks, Deo Gratias; *Penitence:* My eyes are dim with weeping, Be still and know; *Scripture:* Hallelujah, There is one among us; *Concern:* Bring your best to their worst; *Commitment:* In love you summon; We will take what you offer; *Leaving:* The peace of the earth.

G-5111 Music Collection • 96 pp
CD-460 Compact Disc • CS-460 Cassette

ONE IS THE BODY

A new collection of songs
Songbook/CD/cassette
Wild Goose Worship Group

The identity of Christians is intimately tied up with what they sing. Hymns and songs affect our understanding of the width or narrowness of the Gospel, whether faith is couched in archaic language or reflects contemporary culture and whether the church is essentially monochrome or mosaic. The identity of the Body of Christ is thrown into new relief when we realise that the presumed complexion of the Church is no longer white and affluent, but black and poor.

This has compelled the Wild Goose Resource Group to ensure that, in its work with church music and musicians, as broad a panoply of material as possible is represented. *One Is the Body*, therefore, encompasses songs from places as diverse as Hawaii and the Democratic Republic of the Congo, while also representing the home-grown fruit produced in and around Glasgow. These songs are primarily for congregational use, for it is to the congregation which God directs the commandment: 'Sing me a new song.'

G-5790 Music Collection
CD-513 Compact Disc • CS-513 Cassette

Also from the Wild Goose Resource Group:

Courage to Say No (book), John L. Bell/Graham Maule *G-4244*

Courage to Say No (cass.), Wild Goose Worship Group *CS-369*

Courage to Say No (CD), Wild Goose Worship Group *CD-369*

Enemy of Apathy (book), John L. Bell/Graham Maule *G-3647*

God Never Sleeps (cass.), John L. Bell *CS-348*

God Never Sleeps (CD), John L. Bell *CD-348*

God Never Sleeps (octavos), John L. Bell *G-4376*

Heaven Shall Not Wait (book), John L. Bell/Graham Maule *G-3646*

Heaven Shall Not Wait (cass.), Wild Goose Worship Group *CS-267*

Heaven Shall Not Wait (CD), Wild Goose Worship Group *CD-267*

Innkeepers and Lightsleepers (book), John L.Bell *G-3835*

Innkeepers and Lightsleepers (cass.), WG Worship Group *CS-287*

Innkeepers and Lightsleepers (CD), WG Worship Group *CD-287*

Last Journey (book), John L. Bell *G-4527P*

Last Journey (book and CD), John L. Bell *CD-381P*

Last Journey (cass.), John L. Bell *CS-381*

Last Journey (CD), John L. Bell *CD-381*

Last Journey (octavos), John L. Bell *G-4527*

Love and Anger (book), John Bell/Graham Maule *G-4947*

Love and Anger (cass.), Wild Goose Worship Group *CS-428*

Love and Anger (CD), Wild Goose Worship Group *CD-428*

Love From Below (book), John L. Bell/Graham Maule *G-3648*

Love From Below (cass.), Wild Goose Worship Group *CS-270*

Love From Below (CD), Wild Goose Worship Group *CD-270*

Many and Great (book), John L. Bell (ed./arr.) *G-3649*

Many and Great (cass.), Wild Goose Worship Group *CS-275*

Many and Great (CD), Wild Goose Worship Group *CD-275*

Psalms of Patience Protest Praise (book), John L. Bell *G-4047*

Psalms/Patience Protest Praise (cass.), WG Worship Group *CS-313*

Psalms of Patience Protest Praise (CD), WG Worship Group *CD-313*

Sent By the Lord (book), John L. Bell (ed./arr.) *G-3740*

Sent By the Lord (cass.), Wild Goose Worship Group *CS-276*

Sent By the Lord (CD), Wild Goose Worship Group *CD-276*

Psalms of David/Songs of Mary (octavos), John L. Bell *G-4830*

Psalms of David/Songs of Mary (cass.), John L. Bell *CS-403*

Psalms of David/Songs of Mary (CD), John L. Bell *CD-403*

Seven Songs of Mary (book), John L. Bell *G-4652*

Singing Thing, John L. Bell *G-5510*
Take This Moment (cass.),Wild Goose Resource Group *CS-464*
Take This Moment (CD),Wild Goose Resource Group *CD-464*
Take This Moment (octavos),John L. Bell *G-5155*
Wee Worship Book, Wild Goose Worship Group *G-4425*
When Grief Is Raw (book), John L.Bell/Graham Maule *G-4829*

To order Wild Goose Resource Group titles,

or to request a copy of our catalog,

please contact:

GIA Publications, Inc.

7404 S. Mason Ave.

Chicago, IL 60638

www.giamusic.com

1.800.442.1358

Wild Goose Publications, the publishing house of the Iona Community established in the Celtic Christian tradition of St Columba, produces books, tapes and CDs on:

- holistic spirituality
- social justice
- political and peace issues
- healing
- innovative approaches to worship
- song in worship, including the work of the Wild Goose Resource Group
- material for meditation and reflection